Praise for *Here Goes [Nothing]*

"Kendra writes from the heart about her hilarious attempts to reach out to her neighbors. If you're an introvert like me, you'll appreciate the cringe factor, but also the longing for a world where we are more deeply connected to one another. Truly subversive."

—Craig Greenfield
Founder of Alongsiders International
and author of *Subversive Jesus*

"Richly combining Scripture and sarcasm, Kendra Broekhuis's adventures in neighboring could be read for pure entertainment value—you will be delighted with her witty perspectives on parenting, walking with God, and relationships with Other People. But I must warn you that you can't read *Here Goes Nothing* without being poked and prodded and deeply convicted of your calling to love your neighbor, even if you're '80 percent more comfortable sustaining eye contact while wearing sunglasses.' Introverts like Kendra and even extroverts like me will turn each page with a new appreciation for God's design of our unique personality for His glory, in our homes with the neighbors who surround us."

—Amy Lively
Author of *How to Love Your Neighbor Without Being Weird*

"Kendra puts legs on the gospel and gets us out into our neighborhoods. She doesn't just tell us to be good neighbors; she shows us how, modeling a kind of loving that turns cupcakes into conversations. She also made me gut-laugh multiple times, which earns her some crazy respect. After reading this, I want to bust into her introverted world and make her be my friend. She sees spiritual nuggets in everything from apple crisp to maxi pads, and I love her for it."

—Melanie Dale

Author of *It's Not Fair: Learning to Love the Life You Didn't Choose* and *Women Are Scary: The Totally Awkward Adventure of Finding Mom Friends*

"Ordinary obedience to Jesus isn't glamorous, and it isn't a formula, which is why I so appreciate Kendra Broekhuis's message in *Here Goes Nothing*. Too often, we want something to show for our efforts—a shiny takeaway, or a tidy triumph—which can leave us feeling defeated and alone. Addressing this disconnect, Kendra depicts a more honest picture of faith. Detailing her shortcomings and the lessons born out of them, she invites us into her thirty-day journey of intentional discipleship. Her daily meditations are full of meat but easy to digest, leading readers deeper without weighing them down. This book is 'not a success story,' but it is an encouragement and a helpful guide.

—Sharon Hodde Miller

Author and blogger

"If you are an introvert—no, wait—if you are a person who wants to love your neighbor because Jesus commanded you to but gets overwhelmed at the idea, please read this book. Kendra Broekhuis has given us a gift in *Here Goes Nothing: An Introvert's Reckless Attempt to Love Her Neighbor*. It is relatable, hilarious, honest, and inspiring all at once. I feel both understood as an introvert who treasures people but doesn't always want to be with them and challenged to push through my own awkward to actively love anyway. In a world where we are increasingly disconnected, this book pushes us toward our 'neighbor' in beautiful ways."

—Alexandra Kuykendall
Author of *Loving My Actual Life* and cohostess
of *The Open Door Sisterhood Podcast*

"Wise and funny, Kendra takes you along for the ride on her adventure to love her neighbors. Full of encouragement and practical information, *Here Goes Nothing* is a perfect guide for introverts and extroverts alike."

—Kristin Schell
Author of *The Turquoise Table: Finding Community
and Connection in Your Own Front Yard*

"Kendra Broekhuis's *Here Goes Nothing: An Introvert's Reckless Attempt to Love Her Neighbor* is one of those rare reads that has you nodding your head and smiling throughout. From her description of the Baby Buffer to her #SarcasmFont, I recognized my mom-self on page after page. Kendra is that friendly mom who leaves you feeling happier than when she found you, while she quietly displays Christ's love to all she meets. She left me asking myself, 'How can I be the light of Christ in my everyday?'"

—Kim de Blecourt
Author of *Until We All Come Home: A Harrowing Journey,
a Mother's Courage, a Race to Freedom*; international
speaker and president of NourishedHearts.org

"*Here Goes Nothing* equips introverts like me to love the world that God loves. That's a big win, right? It also gives extroverts a rare glimpse into our curious inner workings. With humor, insight, and courage, Kendra Broekhuis helps us all be the people we were created to be."

—Margot Starbuck

Author of *Small Things With Great Love*

"I love the way Kendra Broekhuis creatively intertwines motherhood with mission! Through her honest and delightful way of looking at life, she offers us a positive way to live every day. *Here Goes Nothing* is filled with inspirational stories and personal reminders of how we can open our eyes to the ordinary and see God working in the midst of our daily circumstances."

—Karol Ladd

Author of *The Power of a Positive Mom*

"I love this book and its authentic approach. Kendra Broekhuis takes us inside the mind of the introverted Christ follower as she learns to engage the people who live right outside her front door. Her self-deprecating humor makes *Here Goes Nothing* easy and fun to read. Kendra reminds us all that taking the first small step is the key to experiencing change. This is a must-read for anyone who desires to make a difference in their community."

—Dave Runyon

Coauthor of *The Art of Neighboring*

here goes **Nothing**

here goes Nothing

an introvert's reckless
attempt to love her neighbor

kendra broekhuis

W PUBLISHING GROUP

AN IMPRINT OF THOMAS NELSON

Published in Nashville, Tennessee, by W Publishing, an imprint of Thomas Nelson.

Thomas Nelson titles may be purchased in bulk for educational, business, fund-raising, or sales promotional use. For information, please e-mail SpecialMarkets@ThomasNelson.com.

Any Internet addresses, phone numbers, or company or product information printed in this book are offered as a resource and are not intended in any way to be or to imply an endorsement by Thomas Nelson, nor does Thomas Nelson vouch for the existence, content, or services of these sites, phone numbers, companies, or products beyond the life of this book.

Unless otherwise noted, Scripture quotations are taken from the Holy Bible, New International Version®, NIV®. Copyright © 1973, 1978, 1984, 2011 by Biblica, Inc.® Used by permission of Zondervan. All rights reserved worldwide. www.zondervan.com. The "NIV" and "New International Version" are trademarks registered in the United States Patent and Trademark Office by Biblica, Inc.®

Scripture quotations marked ERV are taken from the Holy Bible: Easy-to-Read Version. Copyright © 2006 by Bible League International.

Scripture quotations marked NKJV are taken from the New King James Version®. © 1982 by Thomas Nelson. Used by permission. All rights reserved.

ISBN 978-0-7180-8332-8 (E-book)

Library of Congress Cataloging-in-Publication Data

Names: Broekhuis, Kendra, author.
Title: Here goes nothing : an introvert's reckless attempt to love her
   neighbor / Kendra Broekhuis.
Description: Nashville, Tennessee : W Publishing, [2017] | Includes
   bibliographical references.
Identifiers: LCCN 2016040354| ISBN 9780718083267 (trade paper) | ISBN
   9780718083328
Subjects: LCSH: Love--Religious aspects--Christianity. | Service (Theology) |
   Interpersonal relations--Religious aspects--Christianity. |
   Introversion--Religious aspects--Christianity. | Introverts--Religious
   life.
Classification: LCC BV4639 .B8235 2017 | DDC 241/.671--dc23
LC record available at https://lccn.loc.gov/2016040354

Printed in the United States of America

17 18 19 20 21 RRD 10 9 8 7 6 5 4 3 2 1

For Jesus. Who loved me first.
And for my neighbors. Whom I want
to better love in return.

Contents

Contents

Before We Get Started

God does not need our good works,
but our neighbor does.

—Martin Luther[1]

This is not a success story.

And it's not one of those stories that has a beginning, a middle, and then a perfectly tidy ending either. It's really just a beginning.

You see, for thirty days I prayed, *God, help me to maintain the joy of being Wife and Mommy amid the daily grind. To see the world through Your eyes. To live intentionally. To build relationships and share Christ's love with our neighbors. To learn what it really means to give. To collide motherhood with mission.*

This became my motto, my credo, my personal mission statement of sorts.

Some days it led to actions the Lord gently nudged me to take. Other days it led to reflections the Lord gently whispered into my heart. Every day it led to one word, one underlying theme that tied all thirty days—all thirty chapters—and their wide variety of topics together: *giving.*

These thirty days—September 29 through October 29, 2014, to be exact—found us in a strange time of transition. We had just moved back to the United States after teaching for three years in the beautiful country of Guatemala. We were living in a new city, residing in a new apartment building, and searching for a new church. And we wanted to put it all together: all of our experiences, all of the things we had just seen and learned and read and discussed. I wouldn't call it a clean slate—just a chance to live intentionally.

Before we moved back to the United States, we sat down with our dear friends and InnerCHANGE missionaries, Nate and Myra. They gave us guidance to work through our transition as well as our desire as a family to pursue more than our own happiness. When we asked them, "What do we do first?" their answer was this: "Get to know your neighbors."

It might sound like strange advice, but it made sense. Jesus told us to love God and love our neighbor. Many times the word *neighbor* is meant to be vague, but our friends knew that it shouldn't always be. They knew that part of being mission-minded, no matter where you live or work, is being willing to love the people closest to you, people you often overlook. I tell you this because our neighbors—as in the people who lived in the other eleven apartments in our building—were who I often found the Lord's generosity overflowing to and from during these thirty days.

Sitting in the kitchen of our apartment in Guatemala, listening to Nate and Myra's advice, I felt excited, inspired. But one long bus ride to the airport, two flights to the United States, and three months later, the idea of actually focusing our lives on connecting with strangers made me want to dry heave just a little bit.

Like the typical introvert, being around new people for an extended amount of time makes me weary. And when a stranger enters my personal-space bubble, a whole host of physical changes happens in my body. My everywhere begins to sweat. I worry that I need an extra swab of deodorant or a breath mint. My mouth turns to cotton, and from the pit of my stomach emerges a host of butterflies. And if I can get past the physical hurdles of meeting someone new, then I have to get past the mental block of trying to think of a good question to ask, which quickly turns into twenty dumb questions I shouldn't ask.

I mean, the whole scenario is like watching Middle School and Puberty get married and have a baby named Awkward. I can give socializing with strangers a good effort, but then I usually need a prescription of lonely solitude for at least an hour after the ordeal. Which is why when people talk about things like building relationships and sharing the gospel with my neighbors, I would rather take a second and throw up in Baby's diaper bag.

But I'm afraid that at times I let my introversion become an excuse, that maybe I play that card too often. Unfortunately, our technology-obsessed culture is not helping me develop the courage and social skills to look into people's eyes and just say hello. I hover behind my screens instead of being available to those I pass by every day. I avoid relationships that take more work than using my thumbs to text. I say, "Hello, how are you?" and "Good, you?" to our neighbors and never take the next steps to get to know them.

But what if, instead of staying inside my thick, introverted shell, I prayed for courage to step out and build relationships with our neighbors? What if, instead of making a to-do list, I prayed for God to guide my daily activities? What if, instead of waiting for people to knock on our door, I intentionally looked for ways to show Christ's love and kindness?

Here goes nothing, I thought, and so began thirty days of

finding out a few answers to these questions. *What if?* Well, God just might give you a small taste of what it means to recklessly love your neighbor.

Now, a few disclaimers.

Disclaimer #1: I don't believe any generous thing I do can earn my way to heaven.

I believe only the generous thing Jesus has already done can save me, faith in Christ alone.

> For it is by grace you have been saved, through faith—and this is not from yourselves, it is the gift of God—not by works, so that no one can boast. (Eph. 2:8–9)

I believe that giving is part of the answer to "Now what?" As in, *I believe in You, Jesus! But now what?* Because right after the verses about God's grace and our faith, it says this:

> For we are God's handiwork, created in Christ Jesus to do good works, which God prepared in advance for us to do. (v. 10)

Generosity is essential not because I think I can earn my way to heaven but because I have been given eternal life in heaven, for free. I give not out of a futile mind-set of repayment but out of sheer gratitude.

Disclaimer #2: My circumstances are different from yours.

Our situations, relationships, experiences, life stages, histories, husbands, babies, parenting styles, denominations, ages, in-laws, education, houses, bills of health, finances, locations, and methods of wiping our bottoms may be different from each other's. And that's okay; that's great.

I am "just" a stay-at-home mom. My husband is "just" a high school science teacher. At the time these thirty days happened, we had "just" one fourteen-month-old daughter. We lived in "just" a two-bedroom, one-bathroom apartment, and we owned "just" one car and two bikes. While we can't compare lives, I pray we can encourage one another, challenge one another, and cheer one another on, even in our differences.

Disclaimer #3: The resources at the end of each chapter are optional.

I provided reflection questions, actions to take, and passages to read. All are meant to be extensions for anyone looking to take that chapter's concept of giving deeper. But I don't want to be the bearer of unnecessary guilt, unrealistic expectations, or overworked schedules. Use the "To Take This Deeper" resources if that's what the Lord is laying on your heart; don't otherwise. I don't know your life. You do; God does.

Disclaimer #4: This is not an easy, thirty-day plan for how to become a generous person.

Like I said, it's not a success story. And the commands to love God and love your neighbor are not always effortless. It's a lifelong lesson that's about as comfortable to learn as middle school sex ed, and about as easy as teaching middle school sex ed class.

So whether you are making the commitment to read this book one day at a time, one page at a time; by binge reading; or in a book club with your besties, I pray with my whole heart that God will use it to encourage you, challenge you, and cheer you on both to *recognize* His message of "I love you" in the everyday moments of your own life and to *be* His message of "I love you" to the everyday people in your life.

Five Quarters and a Tide Detergent Pod

Give What I Have

*It's not how much we give but how
much love we put into giving.*

—Mother Teresa[1]

Pay for someone's laundry.

It was a fleeting thought, something I could easily push past, ignore, and forget about as I got on with the rest of my morning. But I had been praying again recently. I say "again" because it had been far too long since prayer was a regular part of my day. It was one of those things I easily buried beneath the unscrubbed dishes, stinky diapers, and dirty laundry. I was like, "Prayer? Ain't nobody got time for that!"

I had my moments of being a prayer warrior princess. Like that time when I was giving birth to Baby and cried, *"Just get it out!"* And like that other time when we were going to move back to the United States from Guatemala and we begged God to give Husband a job so we wouldn't have to live with my parents forever. I think that prayer was, *Just get us out!*

But prayer was becoming more than a desperate cry for help. Recently I had been praying for some inspiration from the Lord, for ways I could be more alert to His voice, for inventiveness in how I could share His love with our neighbors.

I believe when people pray, the Lord answers. Sometimes, like the prophet Elijah, I expect God to answer in the great and powerful winds, the earthquakes, and the fires. But sometimes God chooses to speak in gentle whispers (1 Kings 19:11–13).

Gentle whispers, like God saying:

You are wonderfully made (Ps. 139:14).

I will take care of you (Ps. 55:22).

Trust Me (Prov. 3:5).

Remain in Me (John 15:4).

Follow Me (Matt. 4:19).

I love you (John 3:16).

Share My love with others (Mark 12:31).

Give to others as I gave to you (Matt. 10:8).

His tender voice can be heard in Scripture, in prayer, in the wise words of a friend, and in those beautifully ordinary moments of the day that surprise me like an affectionate kiss on the cheek. God doesn't always shout or post billboards or share Facebook memes like I wish He would, but He speaks.

Pay for someone's laundry.

My Monday morning had been extremely ordinary until that point. So far I had vacuumed Sunday's crumbs, washed Sunday's dishes, and planned what I was going to cook for Monday night's dinner. Next was laundry. I had just returned from a nine-day trip to Guatemala and come home to the realization that almost everything made of fabric in our apartment was due for a good washing. I gathered the blue mesh bag bursting at the seams with our dirty laundry with one hand, straddled Baby on my hip with the other, and dragged everything down two flights of stairs to the laundry room. It was while I was dragging and heaving and sweating that this idea brushed my mind.

Pay for someone's laundry.

Now, random thoughts cross my mind all the time. I think it is part of being an introvert. If I'm not going to talk to other people, I might as well talk to myself. *(Am I right, Self?)* Most of the time I just brush it off and go about my day like I'm not crazy, but this thought was different. I decided to stop ignoring and start listening.

Pay for someone's laundry.

Nothing fancy, nothing life changing, nothing—ironically—worth writing a book about. Nothing terrifyingly reckless for my introverted self to do, like speaking words out loud to a stranger. Nothing deeply sacrificial, except donating quarters, of course. It was only twenty-five cents, but now that we lived in an apartment building with coin laundry, trying to find quarters was like trying to mine for diamonds in the parking lot.

While my mountain of laundry was in the dryer, I scribbled on an obnoxiously yellow sticky note, *Dear Neighbor, Please enjoy a free load of laundry. I prayed for you this morning, and I hope you feel Christ's love throughout your day.* Simple. Encouraging. Not too creepy, I hoped.

Next, I needed quarters. After scrounging through the coin jar, my wallet, the car, and the couch, I found only five.

Well, that's extremely lame, I thought. *Five measly*

*quarters? Enough to fill only one of the two laundry machines
and neither of the dryers? Why am I even bothering?*

Give what you have.

The second whisper, and my first lesson. Then my adult
temper tantrum. *But, Lord, I wanted to be able to give more; I
wanted to give enough for two laundry machines and one dryer.
I wanted to give fourteen quarters, not five! And I wanted to be
able to do it* all by myself!

Give what you have.

Sometimes I think things like, *If I can't do it all by myself,
then I'm not going to do it at all.* I let either my pride or my insecurities get in the way of giving. But the reality is, I don't have
enough of anything to do it "all by myself." I'm only expected
to do my part, to give what I have, no shame or pride, no
matter how humble or glamorous it is. God has equipped me
with exactly what I need to accomplish His will. He can still
do great things with whatever I am able to offer up in worship.

I think about that boy and his five loaves of bread and two
fish (Matt. 14:13–21). What if he hadn't brought them forward
when Jesus had a hungry megachurch congregation to feed?
What if he had decided to be a little punk and say, "Well, that's
extremely lame! Five measly loaves and two scrawny fish? I
wanted to be able to give more, to feed all five thousand! *All by
myself!*" First, that's just absurd. Second, the boy would have
missed out on an opportunity to share in Christ's miraculous
demonstration of His power. It may have been a humble offering, but did that make the outcome any less effective, any less
miraculous?

Jesus again emphasized the concept of "give what you
have" to His disciples as they watched people present their
offerings at the temple:

Many rich people threw in large amounts. But a poor widow came and put in two very small copper coins, worth only a few cents.

Calling his disciples to him, Jesus said, "Truly, I tell you, this poor widow has put more into the treasury than all the others. They all gave out of their wealth; but she, out of her poverty, put in everything—all she had to live on." (Mark 12:41–44)

I can't always give a lot, but that is no excuse to keep from giving. I can always give what I have, right now, in this moment, and trust God to provide the rest. My time, my money, my talents, and when I'm really feeling it, my mojo. Some days it might be enough to buy two loads of laundry and feed five thousand; other days it might be less.

I stuck the five quarters in the washing-machine slot and weighted the sticky note with a Tide detergent pod. Throughout the rest of the morning I kept the promise I wrote on the sticky note. I prayed this gift would bless whoever needed it most in our building, and for the discovery to be timed in a special way that would point him or her to Jesus. Maybe I was expecting too much out of five quarters and a Tide detergent pod, but I figured if they weren't meant for performing some sort of miracle, at least someone else in our apartment building might appreciate not having to mine for quarters in order to wash his or her laundry.

I gave what I had that day, but I probably learned even more. The funny thing is that the quarters likely were not mine. Chances are they came from a butter tub of quarters my dad gave us when he learned we had to do coin laundry in our new apartment building. And the Tide detergent pod definitely wasn't mine—or at least not originally. My mom gave me a huge box of them when we moved. (My parents, I love them. Also, they think we're poor.)

But isn't that the perfect reflection of what giving is? Is anything I give actually mine? No, what I give is never my own; what I share is never from what I have created or collected or earned or harbored for myself. What I give is always an overflow of the gifts and the love I have been given in Christ.

I didn't know what the impact of five quarters, a Tide detergent pod, and a sticky note would be. While He is able, I didn't expect God to multiply it into five thousand loads of laundry. But even when I have nothing left to give, I always have a prayer to pray. I can pray it will make a difference in someone's day, pray it will point him or her to Christ, pray it will encourage.

I can pray the Lord will speak into my heart again tomorrow, pray I will be paying close enough attention to hear Him.

To Take This Deeper

Give What I Have

- **Reflect:** Have there ever been times when you chose not to give because you didn't feel like what you had was a lot or like it would be enough? Trust that God has equipped you with the perfect amount of gifts, talents, and money. Trust that He can multiply your gift and use it just as it is to accomplish His work.
- **Take Action:** Pray for God to reveal to you an act of kindness you can do for one of your neighbors.

No matter how random it might seem, listen to God's instruction and follow through with that act of kindness. Pray that the neighbor you give to will be blessed by your gesture, which says, "I care about you."

- **Read:** Read 2 Corinthians 12:9–10. Be encouraged as Paul talks about Christ's power being made perfect through his weaknesses. We aren't enough all by ourselves, but Christ is. Always.

Mulligan Day

Give Obediently

To trust Him means, of course, trying to do all that He says. . . . Not hoping to get to Heaven as a reward for your actions, but inevitably wanting to act in a certain way because a first faint gleam of Heaven is already inside you.

—C. S. Lewis, *Mere Christianity*[1]

I'm not sure why people call four o'clock *happy hour*. Because there is nobody in the world happier than a two-o'clock mommy who just put her child down for a nap. Beverage of choice? One to two hours of peace and quiet.

It was one of those mornings I could have used a tall glass of Mommy Happy Hour. Baby was cutting molars, and I swear she had turned into a monster. I couldn't even get through scrubbing a medium stack of dishes without her desperately crawling up my leg, sobbing some of the most enormous tears I have ever seen.

It's on days like these I usually declare a Mulligan Day. Mulligan Days are special occasions that happen when the morning starts out like the book *Alexander and the Terrible, Horrible, No Good, Very Bad Day.* On Mulligan Days I give up—usually by about 9:27 a.m. I make the conscious decision to take the rest of the day off from any motherly and wifely expectations besides things required for basic survival, like changing a diaper or making macaroni or snuggling a crabby baby. I stay in my sweatpants, turn on PBS, and inhale most of the chocolate we have in the house. Basically, I live out an episode of *Moms Gone Wild* for the rest of the day.

Make some cupcakes for your neighbor.

I heard, but I didn't want to listen. *Seriously, Lord? Cupcakes? Now?* I cried out for mercy instead. *But, Lord, it's Mulligan Day. Can't we agree on something that won't take more than five minutes and a few quarters? You know what Baby is like when she's teething. She is awful. And You want me to play Betty Crocker and make cupcakes? I deserve a break! I'll just try again tomorrow.*

Barf. "Deserve." *Deserve* is such an ugly word. It makes me think somebody owes me something, or even worse, that the Lord owes me something. It makes me think I can keep score, that I can make excuses. That if I endure one hardship in my day, such as Baby teething, I can expect to be gifted with no more hardships the rest of my Mulligan Day. *Deserve* is unbiblical. It makes my heart bitter. It is the exact opposite of Christ's humility.

In your relationships with one another, have the same mindset as Christ Jesus:

Who, being in very nature God,
did not consider equality with God something to be
used to his own advantage;
rather, he made himself nothing
by taking the very nature of a servant,
being made in human likeness. (Phil. 2:5–7)

If I want to use the word *deserve*, I need to first remember that Jesus never sought after what He deserved. He is God but chose humanity. He is King but chose servanthood. He is Almighty but chose obedience. I "deserve" nothing.

With my attitude in check, I took a deep breath and prayed, *Lord, which neighbor? And what message do You want me to send with this random batch of cupcakes?* The neighbors who lived right below us popped into my head. I thought maybe these cupcakes could be a peace offering for all the racket Baby makes through their ceiling every day. Unfortunately, giving someone cupcakes anonymously makes it hard to use them as a two-for-one "We're So Sorry" and "Jesus Loves You" gift.

But here's one funny and noncoincidental thing that made me want to break out in the "Hallelujah Chorus": I had a box of cake mix in our house. We had planned to use it for Baby's first birthday and never did. I said thank you to the Lord for not making me take a special trip to the store with Baby Lucifer. Then I baked: I mixed the powder, eggs, oil, and water; I scooped spoonfuls of batter into muffin cups. And I did it with Baby on my hip, of course, because when she cuts teeth, there is no setting her down. It got all #SuperMom up in here real fast.

I still wondered what kind of message to send until I

remembered that the reason for cupcakes is almost always to celebrate. I wrote, *Hey, Neighbors, You are worth celebrating! You are a beloved child of God, and He loves you so much! I hope you enjoy these cupcakes and feel Christ's love throughout your day. P.S. I prayed for you all morning!* I had no idea if my neighbors needed to hear this, whether or not they needed a pick-me-up, or if they knew Jesus. But this was an act of trust, choosing faithful obedience and knowing God would take care of the rest. No matter how random the task, or how unmotivated I was, or how monstrous Baby was.

At least, that's what I kept telling myself as I waited and waited like an anxious puppy for our neighbors to come home and find the cupcakes outside their door. While I enjoyed the whole anonymous-giving thing, I did not enjoy waiting for the gift to be received. I can't even say the number of times I went up and down the stairs to check on them the rest of the day, because it's a number called Embarrassing. Even after I ran errands later that evening, the cupcakes were still there. The worst part was that their lights were on and someone was home. (No, I promise I'm not the kind of neighbor who should be prosecuted.)

But that was when I went a little haywire in holy conversation with the Lord. *Is this whole pray-and-listen thing a bust? Are You not using these acts of giving like I hoped? Are You just telling me to be patient? Don't You remember I'm not a very patient person? What if they leave the cupcakes sitting outside the door forever until they mold and get nasty? What if the whole building starts talking about the anonymous, molding, Jesus cupcakes sitting in the hallway? What if they aren't taking them because this is South Chicago, not small-town wherever, so people don't eat anonymous food from anonymous strangers because that's a really stupid thing to do?*

Later that evening, Husband asked if I was the one who put the cupcakes outside our neighbors' door. I explained what I was up to, that both the quarters I'd left in the laundry room yesterday and the cupcakes had gone unnoticed so far, and that I felt dumb about the whole thing.

With the careful politeness and political correctness that a husband uses when his wife is in a fragile state, he looked at me and asked, "Are you sure you can handle giving things to people anonymously? I mean, it's only Day 2, and you keep checking on the quarters and cupcakes. And it's driving you crazy."

Yup. Thank you, Polite and Politically Correct Husband. I knew it was true, but as an introvert, this had me conflicted. I liked the idea of easing into this whole giving thing within my comfort zone of privacy. However, that also meant letting go of knowing what happened on the receiving end. Which of those did I want more, and which was I willing to give up? And if my desire was to learn to love my neighbor, were those really the right questions to ask?

My actions were intended to demonstrate faith. Faith acts in obedience and trusts God to take care of the rest. Faith prays before it crumbles into doubt. Faith doesn't worry about success or failure. Faith sets down the dang cupcakes and doesn't look back.

There's a whole chapter in the Bible about faith, about heroes of the faith. Imperfect yet faithful people who chose to obediently give of themselves. People who gave even though "they did not receive the things promised" (Heb. 11:13). Like Abel, who gave the best of his resources as an offering to God. Like Enoch, who gave of his passion to walk with God. Like Noah, who gave up his reputation to build an ark with God. Like Abraham, who gave up his own map to follow God.

> Faith is confidence in what we hope for and assurance
> about what we do not see. (Heb. 11:1)

I'll be honest: it was Day 2, and sometimes this kind of faithful giving was hard for me to comprehend taking on. Give? Give *more*? Give beyond the time and energy I already put into caring for Baby, our bellies, and our apartment? Didn't I have enough pressure on me to keep a home that looks like Pinterest threw up all over it and a body that looks like LA Fitness CrossFitted all over it? Pressure to make enough money to afford Disney World before we retire? Pressure to record every minute of our child's life with pictures worthy of *Vogue*? Pressure to serve organic, free-range chicken with kale-mango smoothies every night lest we choose cancer? Pressure to pretend that I do it all, *all by myself*?

Life as we know it in the United States of America, with all of our white noise and white picket fences and pursuits of happiness, can be a complete energy suck. I mean, I don't even know who the Joneses are that everyone is trying to keep up with, but I kind of want to punch them in the face and yell, "Who can stand up under all of this pressure and actually live beyond it to care for their neighbors?"

I don't think there are easy answers here, but I don't think I'm asking myself the right questions either. I don't think it's about *more* time and energy and love, just *different*. Just *redirecting* what has gone so far off course from a gospel-centered family life that we need to take a step back and remember we aren't here to serve ourselves.

Maybe it's time to let some of those unrealistic expectations go. Just maybe.

To Take This Deeper

Give Obediently

- **Reflect:** Have you ever been discouraged because you didn't get to reap any benefits from the kindness you gave? Have you ever chosen not to obey something you knew God was asking you to do because it felt like too big of a sacrifice? Remember that obedience to God is key in giving—obedience not out of guilt but out of the sheer joy of serving Jesus.

- **Take Action:** Is there something you feel God is asking you to give, but you are hesitating to do so? Maybe it's stuff you are hoarding, time you are wasting, or talents you aren't sharing. Write it down, and pray God will give you the strength to carry out that act of sacrifice, no matter how small or large it is.

- **Read:** Read Hebrews 11. Be inspired by the ordinary, sinful, broken, young, old, yet obedient men and women God used to take part in His extraordinary will.

Introverts Unite!

Give Through Relationship

*Introverted seekers need introverted
evangelists ... introverted seekers need to know
and see that it's possible to lead the Christian
life as themselves. It's imperative for them to
understand that becoming a Christian is not
tantamount with becoming an extrovert.*

—Adam S. McHugh, *Introverts in the Church*[1]

"Introverts unite! Separately! In your own homes!" That is a
real T-shirt slogan, and it has my name written all over it.

I exist somewhere on the introvert spectrum between
Cave-Dwelling Hermit and Hipster Youth Pastor. I like people
most of the time—until I don't like them anymore, which is
usually after four hours of interaction. Less time if "people"
equals "complete strangers."

So when I read words in the Bible like *tell* or *proclaim* or
preach, I feel slightly anxious, a little fatigued. I am someone

who feels the deep joy of the Lord when I get past the part of the church service where I have to shake people's hands. I would be much more comfortable sticking to T-shirt slogans that do all the Christian speaking, interacting, and evangelizing work for me. Maybe they would say stuff like, "Let me tell you all about Jesus! Via text message!" Or, "I am fearfully and wonderfully made to be at home in my pajamas watching Netflix."

Sometimes my introverted tendencies make me question how my personality meshes with getting to know my neighbor, sharing the gospel with my neighbor, or loving my neighbor. But thankfully, new methods for social involvement with strangers are being developed to help introverts like me. My personal favorite is called the Baby Buffer.

You see, when you walk around with a baby, you are never in the spotlight. Nobody, not even the parents who raised you for eighteen years, cares about you anymore. They want to know what is the baby's name, and how old is the baby, and do you bottle-feed or breast-feed the baby, and how do you plan to educate the baby, and how many more babies do you think you'll have? And, oh! Your baby is *so cute!*

Boom. The introverted parent just survived a ten-minute conversation with a stranger thanks to his or her tiny, drooling Baby Buffer.

As my friend stated, "It's way easier to walk up to someone and ask them what their kid's name is and how old they are, rather than to simply look the parent in the eye and say, 'Hi, what's your name?'" I think everyone has witnessed Baby Buffer: Party Edition, the kind where everyone sits in a circle and stares at the children playing in the middle of the floor for entertainment. The kind where all adults appreciate not having to sustain uncomfortable conversation with their distant cousins at a Christmas party.

Using the Baby Buffer method is what helped me meet my neighbor Joan on Day 3.

I had just made a grocery run and was struggling to get everything inside our building, up two flights of stairs, and into our apartment. I usually have to coax Baby to walk across the parking lot herself while I haul the groceries and then sprint the bags upstairs before Baby can knock on somebody's door, steal a welcome mat, or crawl up the stairs and fall down again. That day, as I was frantically running up and down, Baby toddled over to the laundry room where Joan was washing her clothes.

"Where's your mommy?" I heard Joan say.

I ran to the laundry room, sweating and out of breath. "Here I am!" I had never officially met Joan in the month we had lived there, but one time when I went to get the mail, her son-in-law was trying to get in the building. I let him in, and he yelled into Joan's open apartment door, "Ma! I rang the bell, but you didn't have your hearing aids in! Some girl let me in the door!"

Now I introduced myself, and Joan did the same.

"I'm the old lady in the building," Joan said with a laugh. She indeed looked older, with leathery skin and curly white hair. She had hands full of wrinkles and eyes full of stories.

Baby worked her Baby Buffer magic as she ran around the laundry room; Joan was completely enchanted by her. It turns out she had seven babies of her own. I filed that information as Baby Buffer material for future conversations.

After exchanging a few more pleasantries with Joan, Baby and I went up to our apartment. But I wasn't satisfied;

as uncomfortable as I feel around new people and in new situations, I felt more uncomfortable leaving Joan in the "Hello, how are you?" "Good, you?" stage. I knew this was God stirring my heart, whispering for me to go back, to pursue company with Joan, to break the iceberg of awkwardness a little further.

I noticed we still had cupcakes left from baking the day before. I put a few on a plate and remembered that in those rare times I don't have a Baby Buffer, a Food Buffer is my next best option, as in, "Hey! I brought you some cupcakes to reconcile for how uncomfortable I am making you feel right now!"

As I walked across the hall and down the stairs, I prayed, *Lord, please let her have her hearing aids in.* I also prayed she would welcome us into her apartment. I prayed it wouldn't just be a handoff of cupcakes, a "Have a good day," and a shutting of the door in my face. *And, Lord, please help me not be a big, awkward duck. Amen.*

He said yes. I didn't even have to knock on Joan's apartment door, because she was in the community laundry room—"Washing thirteen blouses!" she told me later. When she finished her laundry, she invited us right into her apartment. In the fifteen lovely minutes we spent chatting, I found out she has a cottage in Michigan, the *Sit and Be Fit* workout DVD, and the gift of sarcasm. We are kindred spirits, I think.

Baby made herself right at home, running circles around Joan and me. "Where did she go? She is so fast!" Joan said. She didn't worry about her stuff being ruined, just about Baby hitting her head on the edges of the coffee table. She gave Baby her small exercise ball to keep: "I used it all last year, but I can't find the exercise DVD anymore." And then she even invited us back to her apartment the next day to visit with her friend. "She would love to see Baby!" she told me.

Before we left I asked Joan if I could pray for her. She asked, "Are you the girl who left the change in the laundry room? I didn't take it because there are so many neighbors and your note didn't say which one it was for!"

I laughed and said she missed out on a free load of laundry. And I felt comforted that someone had found the quarters sitting there.

I told Joan I would pray for her and that we would be back the next day to see her and her friend. As we climbed the stairs, I felt like I might need a few hours of silent reading time to recover from all the interaction, but I also felt all kinds of happy after really meeting Joan.

It was humbling, doing something where I couldn't claim any power or skills or charm. It was the perfect comfort that while God designed me with different strengths, He is perfectly able to work through my weaknesses too. That if I am willing, He will use me, whether it's for the kind of work He designed to flow naturally from my hands and heart, or the kind of work that makes me feel all clammy and uncomfortable inside. He will use me as I am, and I am totally cool with being an introvert.

It reminds me that Moses and Paul, both important leaders of God's people, claimed zero public-speaking charisma. Moses begged God to send someone else to do his work until he was finally given Aaron as a wingman to speak in Pharaoh's courts. And Paul often gave a disclaimer to the people he shared the gospel with, telling them he was not eloquent or wise, only weak and afraid.

I didn't proclaim the gospel with words today, but I am praying for relationships, for opportunities. I'm praying that the light of Christ within me will shine to the people I share a roof with. It might not always be easy; with my personality it might not always feel comfortable. It might even require a Baby Buffer, or a plate of cupcakes, or a wingman like Aaron.

Or it might just require an extra prayer for courage.

To Take This Deeper

Give Through Relationship

- **Reflect:** What are your spiritual gifts and areas of weakness? What are some ways God has worked through your weaknesses to demonstrate His power? God designed you. He can use your gifts *and* work through your weaknesses.
- **Take Action:** Let your Christ light shine through loving relationships. Use hospitality, such as an invitation to dinner or a cup of coffee, to start building relationships with the people you know but don't really yet *know*.
- **Read:** Read 1 Corinthians 12. Be confident as part of the body of Christ to use your gifts, not hide or shy away from them.

Four

Instead I'll Say, "I'll Be Thinking About You"

Give Prayer

*Prayer does not fit us for the greater
works; prayer is the greater work.*

—Oswald Chambers, *My Utmost for His Highest*[1]

Kendra, sorry. Went to Michigan to close the cottage. —Joan

That was the note I found on my neighbor's door the next morning, and that was not what I expected. I was expecting to kill an hour of our morning with Joan and her friend downstairs after she had so kindly invited us over. I had made sure to bring Joan's exercise ball for Baby to play with, and I had even made sure not to show up right at 11:00 a.m. so she wouldn't think I was too desperate.

The day before, Joan had mentioned she might go to her cottage, but I didn't put it together. Chalk this up to the memory of two women, one who should maybe be on Life

Alert and the other who daily suffers from Mom Brain. I was disappointed, but moping the rest of the day would not change the fact that Joan was in Michigan and I was in Illinois.

Pray for Joan.

Oh yeah. While Baby was running circles around us, I had told Joan I would pray for her. I'll be honest: I've made a lot of "I'll pray for you" promises I never kept. One time I actually admitted to a friend that I had stopped saying, "I'll pray for you" and replaced it with, "I'll be thinking about you" because I thought it was a more truthful statement.

Consistent daily prayer is so terribly underrated, so easily overlooked, yet so essential. I've mentioned a few of my Prayers in Distress—those big moments when I was giving birth or we were looking for a job. The kinds of prayers we pray when we are standing at a difficult crossroads and begging for direction, or the kinds we cry out when we feel desperate, alone, or anxious. God welcomes those prayers; He listens to them.

> In my distress I called to the LORD;
>> I cried to my God for help.
> From his temple he heard my voice;
>> my cry came before him, into his ears. (Ps. 18:6)

But I don't think those are the kind of prayers that I take for granted. I'm talking about the kind of prayers where I talk to God about all the things He already knows but wants to hear from me anyway. The kind that is a tribute to how I rely on Him for everything I need. The kind where I start and end my day unburdening myself, placing myself in His hands, and remembering that His grace is sufficient when I am not enough. The kind where no matter the circumstances I find myself in, I can rest in gratitude as He provides exactly what we need for whatever lies ahead. The kind that Jesus, even in the thick of His ministry, demonstrated so well, reminding me that prayer is too important to put only at the end of a well-planned agenda. An everyday ministry of loving others starts with prayer, with the Spirit's moving and direction.

> But Jesus often withdrew to lonely places and prayed.
> (Luke 5:16)

That's the kind of prayer I often neglect, the daily kind that is more like a relationship with God than a 911 call. The kind that helps me remember that when the world around me is shifting sand, there's still a rock underneath to hold me steady.

And for those reasons I created a pretty prayer wall in our apartment. I wanted a visual reminder to pray every day. I decorated and framed card stock with swirly, colorful letters: *P-R-A-Y* for Praise, Repent, Ask, and Yield. Excerpts from the Lord's Prayer and supporting Scripture surround it to create one big collage. It's like my HGTV badge of Christianity, because there's nothing Jesus People love more than spiritual wall art and cheesy acronyms. I realize the prayer wall has the potential to be a ticket for a guilt trip when I look at it, remember to pray, and choose to do something else I deem more important with my time, but as a mom raised by another mom, I know the power of guilt trips.

Let me explain each section of the prayer wall:

Praise

> "Our Father in heaven,
>   hallowed be your name." (Matt. 6:9)

> Praise him for his acts of power;
>   praise him for his surpassing greatness. (Ps. 150:2)

Basically, praise is like my cordial hello. It's how I hold off from just showing up with a long list of demands. It's how I stop and remember that God is bigger than my own circumstances, that He is most worthy of my praise. So I praise Him for whatever comes to mind that day. For the birds and the trees, for sunscreen that smells like coconuts. I praise Him for getting my tired butt out of bed in the morning, or for allowing me to put that same tired butt back in bed at night. I praise Him for another breath of mercy to get through another moment of the day. Sometimes I write these praises down on sticky notes and put them on our prayer wall, but praise doesn't always express itself through words. Sometimes it's reverent silence. Sometimes it's hot tears. But it's always full of gratitude.

Repent

> "And forgive us our debts,
>   as we also have forgiven our debtors.
>   And lead us not into temptation,
>   but deliver us from the evil one." (Matt. 6:12–13)

If we confess our sins, he is faithful and just and will forgive us our sins and purify us from all unrighteousness. (1 John 1:9)

While praise lifts God up to the pedestal He deserves, humbly saying sorry for my sins jump-tackles me off the pedestal I like to set myself on. I confess Jesus as Lord, but that doesn't mean my choices never contradict that confession. So I ask for grace: God's generous forgiveness that not only washes me clean but also allows me to come to Him with confidence in realizing that's how He sees me—cleansed, justified, and deeply loved.

I then note the clause "as we have also forgiven our debtors." I don't forgive in order to receive forgiveness, as if I'm trying to earn brownie points. I seek to forgive others because grace-receivers are grace-givers in return. Offering forgiveness demonstrates the change that grace has made in my own heart.

Finally, I take Christ's advice to pray, "Lead us not into temptation," because I have been taught that avoiding sin goes beyond making good habits, writing the perfect resolutions, or simply being clever. Praying this prayer, to be delivered from Satan and evil, recognizes that my own willpower is not enough to resist the Devil's schemes.

Under the "Repent" section are sticky notes with all my juicy secret sins I display to make visitors feel uncomfortable. Kidding. Not kidding. (Want to come over for dinner?)

Ask

"Give us today our daily bread." (Matt. 6:11)

If we ask anything according to his will, he hears us. (1 John 5:14)

This is where I grew up spending most of my prayer time—asking God for things. The "Ask" section has the most sticky notes of different prayer requests, but I'm trying to unlearn what has become my typical session of demanding things I think are best for me, myself, and the entire Milky Way galaxy. I still lift up all of my anxieties, I still cast all of my cares into God's capable hands, but I also try to remember that "daily bread" means God providing exactly what I need to get through the day and the same for any family, friends, or neighbors I'm praying for too.

Yield

> "Your kingdom come,
>   your will be done,
>   on earth as it is in heaven." (Matt. 6:10)

> Many are the plans in a person's heart,
>   but it is the LORD's purpose that prevails. (Prov. 19:21)

The "Ask" section naturally links itself to "Yield." The verses mention "Your [God's] will" and "the LORD's purpose," which again reminds me that God's purpose is greater than my own ideas and desires. When I confess Jesus Christ as Lord of my life and say, "I believe God is sovereign and knows best," then the prayer "Your will be done" is what best follows all of the requests, anxieties, and desires I lay before Him. The "Yield" section has just three sticky notes: that His will be done, that our desires will align to His will, and that we will be given wisdom for our actions and decisions.

Now, there are some days *I can't even* because of the noise, the chaos, and the "I'm too tireds." But I need to be reassured of a few things:

God understands the stage of life I am in. I am a mom, and I'm pretty sure God delights in that—watching His child care for another one of His children. While I am constantly on my knees, it's usually to chase Baby, read books, or play hide-and-seek. But prayer does not always have to happen on my knees in a dark room all by myself. Prayer can be a constant conversation, as between two friends, during any moment of my day: dishes, cooking, driving, even while I'm going to the bathroom with Baby staring at me.

I make time for things that are important to me. That, or I redirect my time from something else to fit it in. Just ask my college self, who dropped an entire hour of studying every Monday night to watch *The Bachelor* with friends. Watching "just one more episode" or scrolling through my phone—posting, stalking, liking, and hashtagging—are just a few instances where my "I don't have time" excuse could more honestly be called "I don't want to make time."

If I "think about" people like I promise, then I can pray for them. It's simply a matter of turning those "I'll be thinking about you" thoughts into prayers. An example: *I wonder how our neighbors are doing with their newborn* turns into *Lord, please bless our neighbors with patience, joy, and rest in the train wreck called Baby's First Month of Life.*

Pray for Joan.

Although today was not what I expected it to be, I took God's instruction to heart and kept my promise to pray for Joan's trip. *I wonder how Joan's trip is going* turned into *Lord, please be with Joan on her trip to Michigan. Give her strength to do the work she hopes to accomplish at her cottage. Bless the time she spends with her family. And protect those fragile hips of hers.*

As I continued to think about Joan, my prayers redirected too. I prayed for any broken relationships in her life to be mended. I prayed she would know Christ if she didn't already. I prayed she wouldn't be lonely but would experience love from her family and the people around her. I want people to know when I offer to walk alongside them and lift up their greatest joys and worst anxieties before the Lord, they can rest assured it will happen. I want them to know they aren't alone, that even when they don't know what words to pray, there are others praying for them.

I can't always give large chunks of uninterrupted time to prayer, but it's not about being long-winded or fancy. It's about relationship, about turning those "I'll be thinking about you" promises, His praise, and my apologies into a constant gabfest with the Father. It's about recognizing the privilege it is to spend time in His presence.

Prayer is essential, and it's powerful. It's the one thing I should do before anything else and the one thing I can do when all else is done.

To Take This Deeper

Give Prayer

- **Reflect:** Do you ever feel too busy, too worried, or too burdened to pray? Remember that even in the thick of His ministry Christ took time to pray, that He understood the importance of fellowship with the Father.

- **Take Action:** Instead of thinking about someone, turn those thoughts into prayers. Pray specifically for your neighbors today: their physical, emotional, and spiritual needs.
- **Read:** Read Matthew 6:5–14. Soak up Christ's simple yet complete model of prayer. God doesn't expect babbling prayers, because He "knows what you need before you ask him" (v. 8).

Déjà Vu and the Car That Wouldn't Start

Give It a Go

We must cease striving and trust God to provide what He thinks is best and in whatever time He chooses to make it available. But this kind of trusting doesn't come naturally. It's a spiritual crisis of the will in which we must choose to exercise faith.

—Charles R. Swindoll, *Jesus: The Greatest Life of All*[1]

I just witnessed a miracle.

I was playing with Baby outside on the playground, which is code for "watching for cars as she climbs over curbs in our parking lot." And then a man came out from the apartment building right next to ours. After tossing a few bags of trash in the Dumpster, he got in his vehicle.

Click-click. No turnover.

Click-click. Sputtering and whirring.

Click-click. His car was dead, and I had a case of déjà vu.

I had seen this happen a few weeks ago when I took Baby out for a stroller ride. A few parking lots down from ours, a different neighbor was struggling to get his car started. I had debated with myself: *Do I go over there? I have a functioning vehicle and some jumper cables in the back to help him out. That is, of course, assuming his car needs a jump start. I am no mechanic.*

But I got nervous. Going over there would have meant talking to someone I didn't know and possibly making a moron out of myself, as I also know nothing about cars. I could have easily used the Baby Buffer method in that situation, as in, "Hey, Stranger, this little cutie right here noticed you are having some car trouble!" But I debated with myself too long and pushed the stroller past the parking lot without stopping.

I told God no. I had prayed for God to open my eyes to see where I could be His love to our neighbors. He answered me and showed me, but I said, *No, not this time, Lord. It makes me uncomfortable. You will have to recruit some of Your extroverts to do that kind of stuff.*

I know it's okay for me to feel peculiar in new crowds and around new people. I know the body of believers needs all types and that the eleventh commandment is not, "Thou shalt becometh more sociable, thus says the Lord." But the fact that I allow my introverted personality to keep me from lending a helping hand because it requires human interaction *is* flawed.

That's the thing about the commandment "Love your neighbor." Those situations aren't about me and my fears; they're about my neighbor and his or her needs. Especially because in that situation I had the car and jumper cables my neighbor may have needed. But I had chosen the easy path. More accurately, I chose the sidewalk that quickly took us in the opposite direction. I chose to let my fears and discomfort win. I chose not to help.

Anyone, then, who knows the good he ought to do and doesn't do it, sins.

The Lord placed a bomb on my lap in the form of James 4:17, and that stung just a little.

I need to talk about guilt for two seconds. The word *guilty* has become taboo among Christians. Maybe because we are good at heaping a whole bunch of guilt on ourselves for things we shouldn't feel guilty about, like that one time I fed Baby animal crackers instead of organic applesauce. Or that other time our apartment was a mess and our child was a monster and Husband was out of town, and I didn't "enjoy every moment" of my day.

But sometimes I feel guilty for a reason, for a good reason. And while I don't want the reason I love my neighbor to be motivated by avoiding guilt trips on the Can't-Live-It-Down Train, guilt can be an indicator that something is a little off in my life. I feel guilty when I choose to do something wrong or when I choose not to do something I know is right. Those guilty feelings are my conscience, better known as the Holy Spirit, speaking to me. In this specific situation, I felt guilty because I ignored the Holy Spirit nudging me in the right direction and chose to take a wrong turn. I could continually ignore the Holy Spirit and those guilty feelings might eventually go away, too, but then I would be right back where I started, living a life of self-centered comfort and neighborly neglect.

I am a slow learner. I have always been a baby-stepper in combining faith with action. My tendency is to want to be a part of God's work until it feels too difficult. I want to be involved enough to be seen in the Instagram pictures and to join in the hashtag campaign on Twitter. But that's it. I don't want to lift more than my thumbs or be stretched beyond my comfort zone otherwise.

Which brings me back to James 4:17: *Anyone, then, who knows the good he ought to do and doesn't do it, sins.*

Which brings me back to watching a second neighbor and another car that wouldn't start, listening to the urging of the Holy Spirit telling me to choose kindness this time. I thought, *Okay. Here is my chance to totally redeem myself, at least if that were correct theological thinking. I'll just walk over and see if he needs help. I'll just ask if he needs our car and jumper cables. Here goes nothing.*

Fact: We have one vehicle.

Fact: Husband drove that one vehicle to work that morning due to torrential rainfall. He bikes to school almost every day, unless Baby and I are awake to drop him off, or unless there is torrential rainfall like there was that morning.

Problem: This time I didn't have the tools to help Neighbor #2 like I thought I did.

I don't think my neighbor noticed us staring at him. Sitting in his car, he threw his head back and hands up in frustration. I told myself I couldn't help, that I had no reason to go over there, that all the good intentions in the world wouldn't get our vehicle and jumper cables to magically appear in the parking lot. *But where is God in that thinking, dear Prayer Warrior Princess?* I argued back.

I put aside my can-do attitude and remembered there are

some things I can't do on my own, so many things I can't do on my own. *All the things.* But how easily I forget. How easily I am deceived into thinking I can rely on me. That everything I have—my family, education, apartment, car, jumper cables—is mine because I worked hard enough to earn it. It's easy to think I don't need faith when I have a paycheck, that I don't have to believe in God when all I have to do is believe in myself. That I don't need prayer or miracles when science and common sense can solve all my problems.

But there is nothing God can't do. I rely on Him, which greatly alters the perspective I have on "my" stuff and reminds me that even when I am in situations where self-reliance isn't enough, there is prayer, there is faith, and there is Someone who can provide. Someone who isn't limited by human weakness.

So I prayed, *Lord, please let his car start, please let his car start, please let his car start.* At this point I'm pretty sure I looked like Smalls in the movie *The Sandlot*, holding his glove up in the air with his eyes closed, praying at the pop fly coming straight toward him: "Please catch it, please catch it, please catch it."

My neighbor turned his car keys one more time. And there was not even one more *click-click*, just a vrooming engine. A little sputtering and whirring, but still able to get him from point A to point B.

God did it. God started his car. God performed a miracle right before my eyes. I did nothing, nothing besides lifting up a prayer for a miracle. All I did was ask.

I stood in awe, wondering what I should do next, wondering if I should run over and tell him what had just happened. But I debated too long, and he drove away.

I thanked God. As strange as it was to pray, I thanked

Him that our car and jumper cables weren't around so I could see this miracle. Sometimes it's not in my abundance but in my poverty that I can finally see God's miraculous provision. Sometimes it is when I take off my rose-colored, self-sufficient glasses that I am finally able to see who is behind it all. I can then see who provides and takes care of us, who has the power to give and take away, who is able to miraculously give us what we need when we think there is no hope.

Sometimes I think about Joseph, who was first thrown in a pit and sold into slavery by his brothers before he experienced God's miracle of becoming the second-most-powerful man in Egypt. I think of the Israelites, who first suffered hunger in the wilderness before they experienced God's miracle of sending manna from heaven. I think of Rahab, who first witnessed the crumbling of the entire city of Jericho before she experienced God's miracle of salvation for her entire family.

Beyond the stories I've read in Scripture, I also think about the people I have met while living in impoverished places. I think of the mamas I worked beside at an orphanage in Uganda and the friends we lived by and talked to and learned from in Guatemala. I think about how in awe I felt of those Christians so poor in possessions, yet so abundant in joy. I think about how their desperate need to rely on God for everything they needed daily, and God's miraculous provision against their despair, was the root of that joy.

> Truly my soul finds rest in God;
>> my salvation comes from him.
> Truly he is my rock and my salvation;
>> he is my fortress, I will never be shaken. (Ps. 62:1–2)

I depend on God. I need Him to take care of me and sustain me. I need Him to guide me in love and kindness toward whomever I might meet. I need Him to provide for me and for my neighbors, even when it takes a miracle.

To Take This Deeper

Give It a Go

- **Reflect:** In what ways do you think of yourself as self-sufficient? Remember that God is the giver of life and all of its abundance. He is able to provide everything you need, even when it requires a miracle, even if you don't get the miracle you wanted.
- **Take Action:** Pray for miracles to happen in your neighbors' lives, for whatever needs they have. How might God use you to be the answer to those prayers, whether it's physical provisions, offering emotional support, or sharing the gospel?
- **Read:** Read 2 Corinthians 9:6–15. Remember that God is able to provide everything you need to "abound in every good work" (v. 8).

Don't Focus on the Family?

Give and Take

Do you just think about your family, or what
God would have you do with your family?

—Francis Chan, from his sermon
"Don't Focus on the Family"[1]

Nothing ruins plans for Saturday family hiking as much as the weather turning to cold, spitting rain. Our plan was to go to Starved Rock State Park, about an hour and a half from where we live. But I didn't care if Starved Rock State Park claimed to be the number one attraction in Illinois;[2] trying to hike in forty-degree-and-the-flu-waiting-to-happen weather with fourteen-month-old Baby did not sound like the number one best idea for our Saturday afternoon.

We were in the car already, slowly puttering out of town, as we debated whether we should still go. But our plans did not involve just the three of us, so our decision was difficult to make. Whatever we decided would affect the other people we were meeting as well. We had to choose if we were going to suck it up and focus on our friends, who would be up for hiking in any sort of weather, or if we would cancel our plans and focus on our own family, who didn't feel like dealing with imminent whooping cough.

I was sitting in the back of the car by Baby, giving her a bottle in hopes that she would soon fall asleep and nap at least half of the drive. But as a shameless fair-weather fan of all outdoor activities, I was also moping because I did not want to go to Starved Rock State Park anymore. I flashed my angry-wife eyes at Husband in his rearview mirror, reminding him that he had to either call and deliver bad news to everyone else or deal with a wife who would be told no. #RockAndAHardPlace

It was ironic for us to be arguing about this today, because we had a related, even beefier argument just a few nights before: Husband decided to return a phone call in the evening before Baby's bedtime. It was the kind of phone call he knew would take a while, and it was the time of day Baby was her crabbiest. I was so over parenting, and I just wanted a break, or at least the option to tag out for six minutes.

I got angry, and I let him know it. "You're a really nice person, but sometimes I feel like you put other people before us and then I have to be the bad guy who puts our daughter and our family first!"

First, that was really unfair of me to say. I married a kind man whose thoughtfulness for others is what makes him a great husband in the first place. Second, although I wish I hadn't said those words in anger, that statement *was* really fair of me to say. Our family has needs, too, like how I need a six-minute tag-out in the evening and we need to avoid bronchitis on a cold and rainy Saturday.

These arguments bring up an important debate for gospel-centered families who desire to care for one another, but who also desire to spread that loving care outside of one another. Sometimes we pray and wrestle through when it's appropriate to say no for the sake of our families and put our families first. Other times we pray and wrestle through when it's appropriate to say yes and make sacrifices as a family for the sake of others. I use words like *wrestle* and *pray* because I want to admit I will always have questions about how "Love God and love my neighbor" applies to our daily lives and different situations we encounter as a family. But I think that's okay. I think it's better to admit I have questions than pretend I have all the answers.

God clearly tells us to "go and make disciples of all nations" (Matt. 28:19). This command is not just for single people or for married people without children. The Great Commission—which God calls *all* Christians to—requires care and nurturing and time and sacrifice. But families also require care and nurturing and time and sacrifice. Can motherhood and mission actually collide?

Of course. Motherhood *is* mission. Because I'm a mom, the first person I am supposed to introduce to Jesus is my own child. I am raising one of Christ's littlest disciples, and I have to take that work seriously. I ask myself, *Self, how are you purposefully sharing the gospel with Baby? How are you modeling a lifestyle that reflects the command to love God and love your neighbor?*

Don't get me wrong; I can't raise my child and demonstrate the gospel to her on my own. That whole it-takes-a-village thing? That's so true. I think back to my own childhood, to all the teachers, coaches, aunts and uncles, and grandparents in my life. I think back to my parents' friends and my friends' parents. There was an entire tribe who raised me, who demonstrated the gospel in my life. As a parent, I don't have to train up my little disciple alone, but I can't leave the job to teachers or schools or pastors or churches alone either. Whatever I am not teaching or reemphasizing or modeling at home has far less chance of being valued in my child's life. So, yeah, Mommy and mission collide each and every day.

And I also know that if Christ's love is in us, then there is a whole lot of extra, overflowing love to be spilled out to the other people in our lives. Maybe our coworkers, maybe our neighbors, maybe any of the other people we easily overlook. The world around us is so dark. Why not share the Light through our simple yet welcoming hospitality, our imperfect yet loving families, our messy yet full-of-grace Jesus stories? That won't happen if our focus is always inward. That won't happen if we never invite people in or never go out as a family to share the love that abounds because of Christ. It's not about promoting ourselves as a precious little Jesus family; it's about promoting Christ through our actions together as a family.

In his sermon appropriately titled "Don't Focus on the Family," Francis Chan said it well:

> We have to be careful that our lives aren't just focused on marriage, but that our marriages are focused, and focused on the mission of what God has called us to do. Because at the end of our lives we could have a wonderful, happy marriage, but at the end of our lives, God is not going to say, "Well done." That is not what He asked us to do. He is going to say, "Well done, good and faithful servant" to those who did what He asked them to do.[3]

It makes me wonder what uncomfortable stuff these commands could lead to. *Um, Lord? Is it okay if I can keep my privacy, though? My safety and security? I would appreciate it if You wouldn't make me take risks or do anything to deplete Baby's nonexistent future college funds. Really, if we could just avoid giving and making sacrifices altogether, that would be awesome. Your will be done, Lord!*

I've been encouraged by knowing all sorts of moms not afraid to get uncomfortable for the sake of loving God and loving their neighbors. Moms whose daily sacrifices are teaching their children the beauty of loving service in a country of entitlement. Moms who allow God to interrupt or uproot their lives in whatever ways He has planned, and moms who find contentment in staying put when that's the assignment they have been given. Moms who pray for wisdom to say yes and no. The splendid thing is that carrying out the Great Commission happens in all places and looks different for every family; the hard thing is that it never happens without effort or intention. Loving others never happens without sacrifice.

I'm brought back to our car, back to me fuming in the backseat as I gave Baby a bottle, back to the beef over whether we should go hiking in the spitting rain. Husband looked at me in the rearview mirror and repeated what I so strongly threw at him a few nights before: "You said that I'm a really nice person, but sometimes you feel like I put other people before us. That you have to be the bad guy who puts our daughter and family first. Today I think we should cancel this trip and go home. I don't want to make you feel that way, and today I want to put our family first." It must have been the Lord who spoke into his heart to guide us. Either that or my angry-wife eyes.

The other people we planned to meet up and hike with

were very understanding when Husband made the phone call. I felt pretty sheepish about it all; not about our decision but how I handled the situation. I prayed my words wouldn't keep us from sacrificing as a family in the future.

We said no as a family that day. Considering our child's physical health made it easier to do, but we have given both yes and no answers in this young-family stage of life we find ourselves in. I think about how we schedule everything around naps and early bedtimes, where many days it takes our whole beings to survive until 7:30 p.m. It's tempting to think that this stage of life is a limitation that holds us back from our full potential of ministry as a family. But God loves to use us where we are. Our child isn't a limitation but rather our first ministry. And she's also in ministry *with* us.

On a lot of days the Great Commission in our lives might look like a teacher going to work while his wife stays home to care for their child. Other times it might look like tag-team parenting while one sits down at her computer to type a book. Other times it might look like loading everyone up to go somewhere, and still other times it might look like inviting people in for coffee, or for dinner, or to stay awhile as they get back on their feet. Sometimes it looks like saying yes; sometimes it looks like saying no.

The Great Commission is not about missions *in spite* of family; it's about missions *as* a family. It's about recognizing that serving together not only disciples others but disciples our own hearts too. So we focus on the time and care and nurture our families need to grow and thrive in Christ, but we also focus on our mission *as* a family, of making disciples both within and outside the walls of our homes.

Because if not us, then who?

To Take This Deeper

Give and Take

- **Reflect:** Do you think just about your family or about what God would have you do with your family? What qualities does your stage of life offer that allow you to serve both the people within and outside your home? Remember that your stage of life and the people in your life are not limitations to ministry; they are your first ministry. They are in ministry with you.
- **Take Action:** Pray as an individual, as a couple, or as a family about how you can make sacrifices to serve people outside your home, whether it's by going out or inviting in.
- **Read:** Read 1 Corinthians 7:27–35. While it might seem like Paul is just hating on marriage, find joy while living in "undivided devotion to the Lord" (v. 35) as you are: Single. Married. With children. Young or old.

No Bleachers, No Bench

Give Together

From him the whole body, joined and held together
by every supporting ligament, grows and builds
itself up in love, as each part does its work.

—Ephesians 4:16

Let me start out by saying that nothing makes me hate church more than shopping for one. Church shopping is *the worst*. (Side note: I don't actually hate church.)

We had lived in our new town for a short time. In my highly unrealistic brain I thought, *This Sunday we will wake up, search for a church on Google Maps, and be blessed to find our dream house of worship. A sign reading* Join This Congregation *will be inscribed on the brick wall, and Baby will survive the full hour of nursery. It will be magical.*

Unfortunately, that's not how church shopping works. Being a church shopper instead requires these three easy steps:

1. Wake up with an incredibly skeptical attitude.
2. Trade in your glasses for a microscope.
3. Inspect *all the things.*

Maybe the hard wooden pew shaves off slivers of your shoulder blades. Minus five points. Maybe the pastor has zero chance of winning *Last Comic Standing.* Minus two points. Maybe the special music performer sings a horrible rendition of "Amazing Grace" that makes your ears cry just a little bit. Minus eleven points.

Church is supposed to be about unity and love and coming together to worship the same God. Church shopping throws that straight out the stained glass windows. I don't care about unity and love; I want to know what makes this congregation better than the one two blocks down the street that has its own version of Starbucks inside. I don't care about coming together to worship the same God; I want to know which praise band is going to make me want to get my butt out of bed, ruin my child's nap schedule, and dress us nicely enough that people will think we are one of those adorable Christian families who has it all together.

There is a horrible kind of selfishness bred from church shopping, but I was trying to find a little good in the process too. Looking for a new congregation in a new city brought up great conversations: discussions about what Husband and I were looking for in a congregation and about what Scripture says are marks of a true church. Hint: it has nothing to do with wooden pews or sermon comedy or Chris Tomlin praise bands. While the search for a new congregation in a new city was a slow process, it felt good to think intentionally about being part of a congregation again.

That Sunday found us in a membership class for a particular congregation we had visited multiple times. Pastors and elders explained their foundational beliefs, as well as expectations for those who chose to become members. Class began with an explanation of their mission statement: "To glorify God through the fulfillment of the Great Commission in the spirit of the Great Commandment." Mmm, that's good stuff right there. "Praise God and preach the good news and love your neighbor." Amen.

Class went on, and I daydreamed in and out. What woke me up and made me pay attention was the fantastic sports analogy the pastor dropped: "Church has no bleachers or bench. There are no spectators watching or players waiting to get in the game. Everyone is expected to participate. Everyone has a divine purpose in how they serve the Lord." #NailedIt

It had been almost a decade since we were participating members of a church, a decade of signing the attendance book as visitors. I had plenty of excuses, like how out-of-state college meant out-of-state church. I attended a lot of different churches on a lot of different Sundays, but any participation beyond that was limited to accepting invites to Sunday dinner for real food not made of pancakes.

And then we lived in Guatemala for three years, and going to church in a foreign country in a language not our own made it difficult to get deeply involved in any way. We just tried to smile and learn the appropriate church lingo, and we got all teary-eyed when a familiar tune was translated into Spanish.

And don't even get me started on how the experience of church changes once you have little cherubs called children. No longer was Sunday a day of rest, no, no, no. Sunday quickly became a day of wrangling an overly tired Baby and being called back to the plague-infested nursery due to our child's incessant screaming. I don't think we are the only ones with the Sunday Struggles either. I swear I hear other parents changing the words to "Jesus Loves the Little Children," mumbling weakly as they walk through the sanctuary doors, "Church is hard with little children . . ."

But the thing called attending church is not the same as the thing called participating. Attending means showing up right on time and slipping out just as quickly. It means not getting involved except for the church potluck when you conveniently forget to bring anything. It means sitting in the same exact pew for X number of years and recognizing only the faces that sit on "your side" of the sanctuary. Attending means no commitment, no accountability, no relationships or community. It's an introvert's dream, really, trying to do church without the whole people aspect of it. But that's not exactly church, is it?

Participating is the opposite, and that is what we are shooting for, a congregation we can participate in.

Everyone is expected to participate. Everyone has a divine purpose in how he or she serves Me.

The elder later added, "We are ambassadors of Christ. Being ambassadors for Christ is not an option; it is an assignment." As mentioned in the last chapter, my first responsibility as a participating church member trying to take part in "Praise God and preach the good news and love my neighbor" right then was to our child.

These commandments that I give you today are to be on your hearts. Impress them on your children. Talk about them when you sit at home and when you walk along the road, when you lie down and when you get up. (Deut. 6:6–7)

So I didn't want the mind-set of "Church is hard with little children" to keep us from attending services during that stage of life, even though we might lose the nursery battle every once in a while. I didn't want the mind-set of "Church is hard with little children" to grow with us as a family into "Church is hard, so why even try?" and keep us from ever getting deeply involved in church: its commitment, its accountability, its relationships and community.

I want to stay in the game always, even though our role and participation as a family will ebb and flow as our family changes and grows through different stages. I want to love the game, even when it is hard and requires a little sweat and pain and getting uncomfortable. Because a church whose members have this all-in mentality, this get-your-head-in-the-game kind of attitude, this we-are-all-on-the-same-team-and-all-have-an-important-role-to-play motto, is something we want to be a part of.

The pastor then gently punched us in the face with this question: "Are you shopping for a church like you would a cruise ship or the way you would a battleship?" In a sense, is our attitude "How will the church serve us?" or "How can we serve in the church?"

Now, in order to be completely candid, I must bring up the fact that I have issues with how serving in the church can sometimes be interpreted as attending a monstrous amount of activities. Church activities have a way of filling up our lives and leaving no space for anything outside our building's walls. Sometimes pastors and members and councils and committees need to just back off and simplify. Accountability is necessary, but I think we can get over the whole "I want to micromanage" or "I want to *be* micromanaged" thing. We're big kids now; God can use our talents and homes and dinner tables for a lot more discipleship than we often give these resources credit for.

And participating doesn't mean trying to do it all either. I'm not going to run the nursery, be on a committee, lead a women's Bible study, and host hymn sings in our living room every Thursday night. I refuse to do a million things half-hiney; I love committing to one or two things with my whole hiney, all in.

But give together. Participate.

The congregation in Acts beautifully demonstrated this attitude of "Let's all participate." They gathered to study the disciples' teachings. They ate meals together and spent time in prayer. They sold their stuff and gave money to anyone who needed it. They worshipped God and opened up their homes to one another. They established a strong community built on the gospel.

"Praise God and preach the gospel and love your neighbor." That's what we were looking for, what we hoped to contribute to. There is a reason the church is called the *body* of Christ: that whole "the ears need the nose, need the eyes, need the butt cheeks" thing. We were meant to work as many parts in complete unity; to participate, not just attend. It will look different for everyone, but that's just different parts of the body serving their different purposes.

> Each of you should use whatever gift you have received to serve others, as faithful stewards of God's grace in its various forms. (1 Peter 4:10)

As the church, in our variety of congregations that span the globe, let's give together. Let's be all in. Let's demonstrate how we are many parts of the same body, how we are a flock with the same Shepherd, how we are branches grafted into the same Vine, how we are brothers and sisters with the same Father. Let's be the team whose players don't just sit on the bench or find a comfy seat in the crowd of spectators.

Put us all in the game, Coach.

To Take This Deeper

Give Together

- **Reflect:** Are you an attendee, or do you participate in the church and its mission: "Praise God and share the gospel and love your neighbor"? Remember that the body needs all of its members doing their parts in order to fully function.
- **Take Action:** It's the seventh day. Rest.
- **Read:** Read Romans 12:1–8. Know that your role in the church, no matter how small or grand or humble or glorious, is important for the body to fully function.

Eight

All I Wanted Was Some "Me Time"

Give Me a Minute

Mother Teresa knew that sacrifice—to be
real—must cost; we must empty ourselves
of something we would rather keep.

—Mary Poplin, *Finding Calcutta*[1]

Me Time.

A Google search defines it: "Time spent relaxing on one's own as opposed to working or doing things for others; seen as an opportunity to reduce stress or restore energy."[2]

Also known as Baby's Naptime.

Synonyms include Happy Hour, A Little Slice of Heaven, Peace on Earth, Sacred.

I use Me Time in a lot of ways: to relax from the day's work, or to actually get the day's work done, or to invest in a hobby that keeps Mommy's brain from turning to rice cereal after hours of peekaboo and "What does the doggy say?" Sometimes I use it for the sweet grace of a hot shower.

I do not like Me Time to be messed with. Hence, the big *Do Not Wake the Baby and Do Not Disturb the Mommy* sign I metaphorically slap on the door of Me Time. Mommies are strong, and we are grateful to be mommies, but we still understand the importance of even five precious minutes of Me Time for the mental survival of this 24-7 job that requires us to be chef, teacher, nurse, coach, chauffeur, maid, tea-party planner, superhero, booger wiper, and so much more.

That day was just another manic Monday, and I was doing all the things I love to hate but are also keeping our family from starvation and yellow fever. Cleaning, laundry, meal planning, and grocery shopping. My agenda involved being home most of the day, so I prayed, *Lord, please open my eyes to what You would have me do today. Show me how I can love my neighbor. Amen.*

Shift forward an hour or so to the laundry room. Somewhere between switching clothes from the washer to the dryer, I felt a whisper.

Knock on the door.

Darn. Um . . . Lord? Should I have more thoroughly explained myself? Should I have said, "Please open my eyes to do only things that won't force me to have face-to-face contact with other human beings?"

God meant Joan's door, right next to the laundry room. Joan, whom I had met the week before and really liked. Joan, who wouldn't bat an eye if we randomly knocked on her door on a Monday morning. But getting over small Introvert Obstacles in the past does not automatically make those same obstacles easier to jump over in the future.

I knew I should knock. It was the answer to my prayer, and I probably shouldn't pray for guidance and then choose to disobey the instructions that are given. After switching the laundry, Baby and I knocked on Joan's door. She didn't answer.

Well, I tried, Lord, I thought. *Looks like I'm off the hook! Thanks anyway!*

Shift forward another hour to Baby's Naptime, aka Me Time. I went to pick up our laundry, and there was Joan, folding our clothes straight out of the dryer. Maybe I should have been creeped out that our neighbor was touching our shirts, pants, and undergarments, but I was so delighted someone was doing my housework for me that I yelled, "Oh my!"

Without flinching, Joan turned and casually said, "You scared the heck out of me."

We chatted for a few minutes, and then she dropped a bomb on me. "Would you like to come in for a bowl of soup?"

Sometimes the Lord works in mysterious ways that remind me that when it comes to the command "Love God and love my neighbor," I am never off the hook. Joan might not have answered the door earlier, but she was standing in front of me right this minute, offering an invitation for us to spend time together *now*. But it was Me Time. While I wanted to spend quality time with Joan, the invitation didn't feel convenient anymore; it felt like it was intruding on my sacred hour of peace on earth.

Knock on the door.

It turns out this direction is not just about the physical act of knocking. It's about waiting for someone to open the door. It's communicating with whoever might be on the other side. It's choosing to be available for an invitation to come in. I stammered out my regrets: "Um . . . no thanks. I . . . uh . . . already ate lunch." I picked up the clothes Joan had folded, threw the rest of the clothes from the dryer into my mesh bag, and went back to our apartment.

Guilt showed up again. Not because I don't ever need Me Time. If I never had even five minutes of peace to rejuvenate from human interaction and motherhood, my child, my husband, and my little world would only know the shriveled-up version of me. But even Me Time can become an idol if I put it before obedience. I folded the rest of our laundry in what was usually the sweet sound of naptime—silence. But the whispering started getting louder:

Knock on the door!

I thought back to the previous week and the acts of secretly giving our neighbors the laundry quarters and the cupcakes. Those were comfortable for my introverted self to do, and my intentions were genuinely kind. Not only that, but giving anonymously is biblical. However, those actions were not going to be the answer to my prayer of wanting to build relationships with our neighbors, because they didn't include *actually getting to know our neighbors.*

If I don't know anything about my neighbors, then even a nice gift like cupcakes made with love and filled with great intentions has the potential to hurt them instead. What if my neighbors are on a diet and those cupcakes are just another temptation to avoid? What if they are deathly allergic to frosting and sprinkles and one glorious inhalation would send them into anaphylactic shock? I am being facetious, but I can't really love my neighbors until I take the crucial step of getting to know them. Who are they? What are their stories? What are their physical, emotional, and spiritual needs? Where and how have they encountered Christ and Christianity before in their lives, if at all?

When we lived in Guatemala, we spent many Saturday

mornings out for breakfast with our neighbor Steve, another expat. We called our time together the Shallow Breakfast Club. We promised to only talk about superficial things, such as Justin Bieber's latest scandals and why Jennifer Love Hewitt hadn't ever won an Emmy, but the conversation always went deeper to the obvious issues of poverty and corruption permeating the beautiful country we found ourselves in. We would always ask Steve, "What do you think would fix these problems? What do the people of Guatemala need?"

And he would always answer, "I don't know. You need to ask *them*."

Though he had been living in Guatemala for more than thirty years, though he was deeply involved in education for impoverished youth, though he was well versed in Guatemala's news and politics, our friend would never claim he knew what the people of Guatemala needed. His policy was that in order to help someone, you need to get to know *him*. You need to ask *her* what she wants or needs. I might have my own ideas on what I think is the best way to help other people, but until I know who other people are, I also have the potential of disempowering them or recklessly hurting them in the process. And that takes time, time spent together and time spent building a solid relationship. That takes forgetting the goal of becoming the helper to the helped and focusing on a deeper compassion that is found in mutual friendship.

Like Jonah, I decided it was better to obey late than not at all, so with the baby monitor in hand, I knocked. I finally knocked, ready to take on the full meaning of *knock on the door*—the waiting, the communicating, the invitation. Joan opened and invited me in. This time I accepted her invitation. We shared a splendid time watching afternoon talk shows.

We chatted about cooking and TV and traveling. I learned new things about Joan too.

She doesn't have a car right now, so she has to wait to get groceries until her son or daughter can take her. Which made me think that one way I could be a good neighbor is to offer to drive Joan to the grocery store or pick stuff up for her when I'm there. And while we were chatting, she said to me, "It's nice to have someone to talk to. Sometimes I go a whole week without talking to anybody." Which made me think that maybe we can watch the *Steve Harvey Show* together and chat about life more often.

Time is precious and limited. But while there are only twenty-four hours in each day, God provides us enough time to accomplish the work He has planned for us. And when I am willing to give, redirect, or sacrifice my time to share my life with others, I might be pleasantly surprised at how their lives have a positive impact on my own. Our neighbors aren't just projects waiting to be fixed or people waiting for us to shove the gospel down their throats; they are people to share our lives with. Paul wrote to the church of Thessalonica not only as people he ministered to but also as dear friends:

> Because we loved you so much, we were delighted to share
> with you not only the gospel of God but our lives as well.
> (1 Thess. 2:8)

Getting to know my neighbor helps me better understand how I can love my neighbor. There are no guarantees they will accept our invitations, no guarantees they will be interested in the gospel we demonstrate through our words and actions. But what if they are?

All it takes to find out is a simple knock.

To Take This Deeper

Give Me a Minute

- **Reflect:** What do you find difficult to sacrifice in order to spend time and build relationships with others? Remember that you can't fully understand how to best love your neighbor until you get to know him or her.

- **Take Action:** Thinking of one of your neighbors you have gotten to know better through giving of your time and relationship, what is one way you could show him or her Christ's love today? Prayerfully consider how you can brighten your neighbor's day with an act that says, "Jesus loves you and I care about you too."

- **Read:** Read Hebrews 10:19–39. Persevere in using precious time to draw near to God and to do good deeds.

Nine

The Name Is Bond

Give Credit Where Credit Is Due

*It is not great men who change the world, but
weak men in the hands of a great God.*

—Paul Hattaway, *The Heavenly Man*[1]

I felt like a creep.

But I had just achieved some sort of 007 James Bond mission without anyone calling the cops on me, so I also felt pretty good about myself. It involved sneaking across the grass to the next building over, placing a note on our neighbor's car, and sprinting back to our apartment, all with Baby in tow.

But let me back up just a little bit.

I had told Husband about the car-starting miracle that happened a couple days before. I was grateful for his wide eyes and smile that said, *I believe what you say, and I don't think you are a crazy person.* But I hadn't been able to get the whole experience off my mind. It had me wondering, *Is the Lord trying to tell me something? Is there something else I should do?* And then I felt the nudge.

Tell him. Tell him what I did for him.

At first I thought it was okay to keep the story to myself, to not share it with my neighbor whose car wouldn't start. That way I would keep good deeds done in secret rather than make this miracle about me and my own decision to pray. But after more thought and prayer, I realized keeping it to myself would be doing exactly that—making the miracle about me and not using it as an opportunity to give Jesus a proper shout-out, an opportunity to point my neighbor to Christ.

That's why I decided to run across the grass to his building's parking lot and put a note with all the miraculous information on his car. I couldn't ring his doorbell because I didn't know which apartment he lived in. I couldn't watch for him through our sliding door because that's called being a stalker. So a note would have to do. (Big win for the introvert.)

But I still felt nervous. For as much Christian education as I have received in my lifetime, and for as much doctrine and scripture and theology as I have digested in class and regurgitated on tests, I am not the poster child for sharing my faith. I have a couple of excuses.

The first is that I came from a place where Christian faith was hip, a smaller city with a reputation for having Christian churches on every corner and Christian schools within every twenty miles and lots of Christian people teaching in the public schools. I grew up surrounded by people who already looked like they had faith, or at least had a similar upbringing, education, and cycle of Christian digestion and regurgitation as I had. And that made it hard to decipher when sharing my faith was even necessary.

The other is that in the rare moments when opportunities come up either to start a conversation that includes Jesus or to add Jesus to the conversation, I freeze. You know how you're supposed to pick either fight or flight in stressful situations? There is definitely a third, unsung category—freeze—that is my approach. I freeze and think stuff like, *What if I talk about Jesus and they think I'm a big dork?* Or *What if I say something about Jesus that really offends them?* It's the topic of shame, really. Like, *What if I feel ashamed because they don't react kindly to what I'm telling them?* But here are a few verses I found when I looked up the word *ashamed* in my Bible's concordance:

> "Whoever is ashamed of me and my words, the Son of Man will be ashamed of them when he comes in his glory and in the glory of the Father and of the holy angels." (Luke 9:26)

And this one:

> I am not ashamed of the gospel, because it is the power of God that brings salvation to everyone who believes. (Rom. 1:16)

And this one:

> For the Spirit God gave us does not make us timid, but gives us power, love and self-discipline. So do not be ashamed of the testimony about our Lord or of me his prisoner. (2 Tim. 1:7–8)

Tell him. Tell him what I did for him.

I had seen this neighbor before but had never talked to him. Our paths didn't cross; rather, they just ran parallel from our side-by-side apartment buildings and parking lots. I didn't know him, his personality, or his knowledge of or past experiences with Christianity. I felt intimidated thinking about sharing the gospel with someone I'd had exactly zero contact with.

But in the membership class on Sunday, the elder had said, "The power is in the message, not the messenger." And it's true: I didn't need to rely on my own power to concoct a great story or speak with enough eloquence that my neighbor would believe. I was only here to share the message, to tell him what God did for him. The pressure was off. So what did I have to fear? What was the worst that could happen? My neighbor might read the letter and laugh at me? He might call and ask me more questions? He might say, "Me too! I believe too!" What was I so afraid of?

Thank goodness for Christ's first disciples, for their examples of courage and actions empowered by the Holy Spirit. They had everything to fear when they shared the gospel: imprisonment, torture, pain, slander, abandonment, rejection, death. Yet they spoke with great boldness—not always waiting for others to ask them to speak.

> Pray also for me, that whenever I speak, words may be given me so that I will fearlessly make known the mystery of the gospel, for which I am an ambassador in chains. Pray that I may declare it fearlessly, as I should. (Eph. 6:19–20)

It's one thing to hold back and keep a miracle to myself as an attempt to do good things in secret but another to do so out of fear or embarrassment or laziness. So I wrote our neighbor a note.

10/7/14

Hey, Neighbor,

I know putting a note on your car is a creepy thing to do. But I have to tell you something. Last week I was playing outside with my daughter, and I saw you get in your car. You tried to start it many times, and it would only click. I noticed your frustration, and was about to walk over and offer to give you a jump with our vehicle, but then remembered my husband had the car at work that day. I was sorry I couldn't help, but then I remembered I could always pray. So I prayed for your car to start, and the next time you tried to start your car, it worked! It didn't click even one more time!

I was so stunned that I watched you drive away instead of running over to tell you. Again, I know this may seem creepy, or maybe it all sounds like a lucky coincidence. But as a Christian, I don't believe in coincidences. The point of me telling you all this is not about me, but to share with you that God is real, He's alive, and He loves you. (Maybe you are a Christian too and this all makes sense. Or maybe you aren't and I sound like a complete lunatic.) But either way, I wanted to share this with you and let you know that I prayed for you again today. I prayed that even more than receiving a miracle of a starting car, you will receive and accept the miracle that Christ died for us—imperfect sinners—and rose again—to conquer death—and wants us to accept Him as our Savior so that we can have life after death with Him in heaven.

I live next door in the neighboring building in Apartment 12. And at the risk of assuming you are not a crazy person—feel free to stop by, ask questions, or come over and tell me why I am wrong.

But I watched God perform a miracle on your car, and I wanted to share it with you.

Sincerely,

Kendra

I looked out our sliding door a number of times to see if he had found and picked up the note from his car. It finally disappeared after dark. I thanked God that he received it and that so far I had not been reported to the police for suspicious behavior.

Lord, You did so much more for him than just start his car the other day. I know, because You did the same for me.

I wasn't sure how the note would be received. I wondered if I was clear enough, thorough enough, whatever enough in what I wrote. If he isn't a Christian, then did the note even make sense? It's easy to forget that all the Christian jargon I grew up knowing might not be common speech to someone who hasn't been going to church all his life. Even words like *sinner* and *Savior* might come across as downright loony.

But this is where God can take over, reveal Himself to my neighbor's heart, and let the note make sense. All I can do is say the words and demonstrate the actions. God has the power to do the rest.

To Take This Deeper

Give Credit Where Credit Is Due

- **Reflect:** What kinds of miracles, provisions, and gifts have you experienced from God's hand? Have you ever ignored opportunities to share with others the amazing things God has done in your life?
- **Take Action:** Whether in quiet prayer, by shouting on the rooftops, or in conversation with a friend, give God the glory (and the credit) for the great things He has done in your life recently.
- **Read:** Read 1 Chronicles 29:10–17. Ponder David's prayer, which gives God the credit for His provisions. "Everything comes from you, and we have given you only what comes from your hand" (v. 14).

Ten

Mom Brain to the World

Give a Hoot

If this is going to be a Christian nation that doesn't help the poor, either we have to pretend that Jesus was just as selfish as we are, or we've got to acknowledge that He commanded us to love the poor and serve the needy without condition— and then admit that we just don't want to do it.

—Stephen Colbert[1]

The cry of a baby always gets my attention. But the cry of my own baby is paralyzing.

I know God wired Mom Brains this way for a reason. We are supposed to care. We are supposed to want to respond to the cries of our own children, to want to help, to want to fix whatever is wrong. It's what makes us good moms. Which is why this game called Cry It Out that we have played with Baby more than once to teach her to fall asleep and stay asleep just might be the death of me.

It had been a rough seven on-and-off months of attempting this method. Our traveling lifestyle didn't help. Getting sick didn't help. Teething *definitely* didn't help. And of course, Husband and me making excuses for why we should go in and pick her up, soothe her, or nurse her back to sleep didn't help either. It seemed like there was always something to keep her from learning this life-altering skill.

I already had low expectations for a long time about Baby's sleep habits, but an entire year of inconsistent sleep brought us all to a whole new level of fatigue, and I was SO. OVER. IT. So over not sleeping more than three hours in a row, so over getting up when it was dark and cold to change her diaper, or to give her medicine, or to nurse her. And I was definitely over the terror that is cutting molars.

I was not fully functioning during the day. I was edgy. I was pretty sure I was getting uglier too. I know parents have mixed feelings about Cry It Out, but I *couldn't even*. I needed sleep. We all needed sleep.

And here I was again: Baby was fighting her much-needed nap as if her crib were a torture chamber on death row, not a wooden frame filled with a comfortable mattress, soft blankets, and an adorable stuffed elephant. And I was unable to focus on anything else, even though I really should have done something to pass the time. But I couldn't relax, couldn't take a deep breath, couldn't get anything done until the crying was done.

I listened to the cries from down the hall. I cringed as the cries got louder or when they got a fresh breath of oxygen. It was as if each shriek were a jab to my own gut. And the moment the crying stopped, it was like being released from the bondage of tears and pain and suffering that both my child and I were going through together in separate rooms.

Released from the urge to jump up and run into the room to save the day, because I knew she needed to learn.

I couldn't ignore my own baby's cries. Even if I had to fight myself not to physically respond, I couldn't ignore them. I still heard them. I still listened. I still felt.

> Whoever shuts their ears to the cry of the poor
>   will also cry out and not be answered. (Prov. 21:13)

I had been praying this prayer for only a week and a half: *Lord, open my eyes to see the world as You see it.*

If only the cries of this world would be as paralyzing to me as my own baby's cries. If only the cries of the poor, the widow, and the fatherless would get my attention and hold me hostage just as strongly. If only I wouldn't feel rested or comfortable or at peace until the world's problems of injustice and greed and selfishness were resolved. If only my senses would be heightened to those directly around me, to my neighbor, to that person I cross paths with often but am too busy to notice. If only I would rewire myself to be a Mom Brain to the world.

If only I lived a life that didn't ignore these cries, because the world indeed is crying out. Crying out for love. Crying out for answers. Crying out to know that beyond their pain, there is hope. And as a follower of Christ, I know where the deepest, most satisfying love comes from. I know where the necessary, most important answers come from. I know where the most promising hope beyond all our pain comes from.

I feel so alone. "Even though I walk through the darkest valley, I will fear no evil, for you are with me; your rod and your staff, they comfort me" (Ps. 23:4).

I feel so drained. "Come to me, all you who are weary and burdened, and I will give you rest" (Matt. 11:28).

I feel so unloved. "See what great love the Father has lavished on us, that we should be called children of God! And that is what we are!" (1 John 3:1).

And I also know Christ asks His people to embody that hope to the world around us. To *be* the kind of love people need now just as much as ever. To respond as Christ's "I love you" when they cry out in their pain and suffering.

I mentioned in the last chapter that my upbringing was filled with an insane amount of biblical knowledge and Christian doctrine. (Shout-out to all the great adults in my life.) But being an active follower of Christ, a disciple who daily takes up her cross and sacrifices her life for the sake of the gospel, means more than knowing Scripture.

> Do not merely listen to the word, and so deceive yourselves. Do what it says. (James 1:22)

How cool would that be, if I *did* Scripture as much as I studied it? If I took the whole Christ's-ambassador thing as a God-given assignment rather than a suggestion? Not just on my T-shirts and bumper stickers but with the actual message of the gospel, with the actual actions of profound love and grace that flourish through the gospel. What if I stressed my inability to ignore the world's cries as much as I stressed my inability to ignore Baby's cries?

Because here I am again, watching, reading, and hearing words like *orphans, refugees, starvation, war, racism,* and *corruption.* And I am unable to focus on anything else, even though the world tells me I should just relax and find something comfortable to do to pass the time, to drown out the cries of the poor and the oppressed. But I can't relax, can't take a deep breath, can't get anything done until the crying is done.

I listen to the cries from my white-picket-fence life. I cringe as the cries get louder or when they get a fresh breath of oxygen. It's as if each shriek is a jab to my own gut. I won't be released from the bondage of tears and pain and suffering that the poor and the oppressed are crying until they are given food for their bellies, justice for their oppression.

I can't ignore the world's cries, not when Christ taught us to pray, "Your kingdom come, Your will be done, on earth as it is in heaven" (Matt. 6:10). And I don't want to ignore them either; I don't want to live comfortably separate. I want my eyes to be opened, to weep and mourn for the devastation around me. I want to enter in and learn true empathy and compassion, to do everything Christ and His ever-miraculous gospel equips us for. It won't be easy or as beautiful as it is to profess; the blood and guts of entering in aren't so glamorous. I bet there will even be days I feel a whole new level of fatigue, days I am SO. OVER. IT.

But what is holding me back? What is desensitizing me to the world's cries? What is making me immune to the shock and desperation and urgency their cries should place on my heart? What lets me listen to a news story about starvation or human trafficking or inner-city shootings and then go back to sipping my hot cocoa like nothing's happening beyond my own little world?

I could blame religion and doctrine and theology and law. Maybe I'm just more interested in *going* to church than *being* the church. Perhaps I'm more interested in being right than being kind, in making everyone think like I do than making sure I love like Jesus did. But it's hard to blame religion and doctrine and theology and law when the God of the Bible says stuff like this:

> Religion that God our Father accepts as pure and faultless
> is this: to look after orphans and widows in their distress
> and to keep oneself from being polluted by the world.
> (James 1:27)

Surely the problem isn't this kind of religion and doctrine and theology and law, or the God of this kind of religion and doctrine and theology and law. I can't blame a God who said that instead of pretending to reverently fast, He would rather see His people make right the injustices of the world, share their food and clothes with the poor, and take care of their own flesh and blood. I don't think the problem is a God who said that all of the law could be summarized by "Love Me and love your neighbor." Maybe the problem is *me*, when I hear the Word but don't heed it, don't take it seriously. When Christ comes back and many people say, "I was in so much pain," will He turn to me and look me in my eyes and state:

> "For I was hungry and you gave me nothing to eat, I was
> thirsty and you gave me nothing to drink, I was a stranger
> and you did not invite me in, I needed clothes and you did
> not clothe me, I was sick and in prison and you did not
> look after me." (Matt. 25:42–43)

I need to continue to pray for my eyes and ears to be opened, that I will be so tuned in to what God sees that I won't be able to ignore the cries of the world, the poor, the oppressed. I want to be as paralyzed by the cries of God's other sons and daughters living in suffering as I am by the cries of the daughter He entrusted to me. I need to realize these cries are God gently whispering into my soul to be Christ's channel of love and peace until it is made right, until the victim is shown justice, the poor are shown mercy, the lonely are shown friendship, the unsaved are shown Christ.

I need to pray to be a fixated, anguished Mom Brain to the world.

To Take This Deeper

Give a Hoot

- **Reflect:** What is desensitizing you to the world's cries? What is making you immune to the shock and desperation and urgency their cries should place on your heart?
- **Take Action:** Pray for God to open your eyes to those around you: the poor, the lonely, and the unsaved. Pray to be His beacon of light and hope to them.
- **Read:** Read James 2:14–26. Take these convincing words to heart. Faith in Christ will produce fruit in your life.

Eleven

Why Apple Crisp and the Fragrance of Christ Smell So Good

Give Because He Gave

Your faithful presence in your situation,
your faithful obedience to Christ, is the
sweet smell of the gospel to those around
you. It may take a day, it may take a week,
it may take a year, but people will notice.

—Pastor Michael Langer, Trinity Presbyterian Church[1]

Is there anything better than apple crisp on a chilly fall day?

Actually, I *do* prefer a cold cocktail while lying on the hot, sandy beaches of Mexico, but that's just my favorite way to spell *vacation*. Apple crisp on a chilly fall day is my favorite way to spell *home*. It feels like warmth and comfort. It tastes like familiarity. It smells *amazing*.

Too bad that eating apple crisp requires cooking it first. If you ask anyone who knows me well or who has eaten dinner at our house recently, you will learn I don't like to cook. Check that: I *hate* cooking. Whenever I search for recipes online, I always put the word *easy* before it. To me, a good recipe has a small ingredient list, a short preparation time, and a large portion yield. (I did not inherit the spiritual gift of being a chef.)

But my friend and I had spent the morning taking Baby to an apple orchard, and now I had a big paper bag of apples I felt inspired to peel, core, slice, and use to attempt to spell *home*.

(Google search: "*easy* apple crisp recipe.")

So who are you going to share it with?

That was the Lord's question that afternoon. That was Him reminding me I can't make a huge pan of apple crisp and think it's okay to keep it all to ourselves; that whenever we have an abundant amount of food, there are eleven other apartments of neighbors who might enjoy a hearty piece. He was stressing the fact that I have been praying to "give a hoot" about our neighbors.

I don't know. Who, Lord? Who should *we share this with?*

I finally decided that Husband could decide when he arrived home from work. Let him be the one to cast lots and pass out plates of dessert.

And then I made the "easy apple crisp" recipe. I rolled it, patted it, and added two extra tablespoons of cinnamon. And while it baked: the smell. *Amazing.* If it wouldn't singe the hair off my scalp and melt the skin off my face, I'd probably stick my entire head in the oven and inhale. Then exhale. Then repeat.

How could something so *easy* smell so good? How could this little act fill our apartment with such a grand, pleasing aroma? I only hoped whoever received this simple gift would be just as blessed eating it as I had been snorting it all afternoon.

And I thought that was possible, because here is what Mary Poplin wrote in her book *Finding Calcutta*, a reflection on volunteering with Mother Teresa and the Missionaries of Charity:

> If you follow the Missionaries of Charity for long, you will find that in their wake everything is left better, whether by their actions or simply their smiles and prayers. . . . Mother Teresa called this "spreading the fragrance of Christ." . . . Mother told the sisters, "Let no one ever come to you without leaving better and happier."[2]

The "fragrance of Christ."

What beautiful imagery: choosing to leave everything better than I found it. Using my actions and giving not only as a fragrant offering to the Lord but also as a way to spread the loving fragrance of Christ to others. It makes sense, comparing our offerings to a fragrance, an aroma.

> For we are to God the pleasing aroma of Christ among those who are being saved and those who are perishing. To the one we are an aroma that brings death; to the other, an aroma that brings life. (2 Cor. 2:15–16)

Just like a spritz of perfume to the wrist or a waft from an open oven door, a fragrance spreads. It doesn't stay confined to the surface area it touches. It builds up, clouds around, moves through the air, and enables others to smell its sweetness.

Follow God's example, therefore, as dearly loved children and walk in the way of love, just as Christ loved us and gave himself up for us as a fragrant offering and sacrifice to God. (Eph. 5:1–2)

Loving. Giving. Sacrificing. A "fragrant offering" to God. And who better to look to as an example of this than our Savior Himself? The One who made it His mission to leave our lives better than before. For eternity, no less. Right before Ephesians 5:1–2, Paul described a few ways we can be imitators of our Savior:

- Speak truthfully.
- Do not let the sun go down on your anger.
- Do something useful with your hands.
- Share with those in need.
- Do not let any unwholesome talk come out of your mouths.
- Get rid of all bitterness, rage, anger, brawling, slander, and malice.
- Be kind and compassionate.
- Forgive.

I don't think this fragrance thing has to be complicated. Leaving someone better than I found them might mean passing on a smile to the man whose face is glued in a perma-scowl. Or using polite words with the frustrating customer-service lady who made it quite obvious she doesn't really care if she solves her customers' problems. Or using my hands to clean up after ourselves at a restaurant, in a store, or at the playground. Any kind interaction or loving gesture applies, any attempt to answer the Lord's gentle *Who are you going to share it with?*

However, simple doesn't always mean easy. (Google search: "*easy* ways to control my temper with the unhelpful customer-service representative.") I am so naturally selfish that it takes a lot of the Spirit within me to unnaturally think of others. *Wait, Lord. I'm supposed to speak* truthfully *about my life and not pretend on social media that I'm living some sort of fairy tale? I'm supposed to watch my mouth and* not *say that word my stubbed toe is burning for me to scream? I'm supposed to* forgive?

Nope. Not easy.

But as I pondered these things, I was brought back to high school, the one where Husband teaches. While walking the halls with Baby the other day, I spotted a poster with their theme for the school year: "Because He did, we can."

> And he died for all, that those who live should no longer
> live for themselves but for him who died for them and was
> raised again. (2 Cor. 5:15)

It's what my life is meant for. To live, not for myself but for Christ—the One who died for me and was raised again. And Jesus preached over and over that one of the best ways to love Him was to love others, our neighbors, the "least of these."

Because He did, we can.

When Husband got home that night, I asked, "Who should we share our tasty dessert with?" He chose our neighbor Jim, who was "Christ's aroma" to us a few months back. The day we moved into our apartment, Jim left a note taped to our door with a Jimmy John's gift card inside. His note read, *Welcome to the neighborhood! Thought this might come in handy on one of those working days when you don't feel like cooking.* It's like Jim knew me before he ever really knew me. Because "You Don't Feel Like Cooking" is the hymn I rap in my head every afternoon at 4:37 p.m.

I was craving a little quiet time, so I sent my slightly more extroverted husband to deliver the apple crisp with a simple message: *Thank you for buying us Jimmy John's (twice!). We enjoyed it again last night. We hope that now you can enjoy some apple crisp!*

Husband visited with Jim for a while. He came back smiling, going on about how cool Jim is and what a great guy he is to talk to. Isn't that just lovely? Two neighbors stinking each other up with Christ's aroma, feeling mutually blessed by good company and good eating. The Lord's gentle *Who are you going to share it with?* turning into His reminder, *See how I also share My love with you?*

I love these excerpts from a prayer by Cardinal Newman:

Dear Jesus, help us to spread Your fragrance everywhere we go. Flood our souls with Your spirit and life. Penetrate and possess our whole being, so utterly, that all our lives may only be a radiance of Yours. Shine through us and be so in us that every soul we meet with may feel Your presence in us. . . . Let us thus praise You in the way you love best, by shining on those around us.[3]

There are times in life that call for big gestures on behalf of others, but many days it's the small stuff that really has an impact. Our faithful presence in the lives of people we work next to, care for, and interact with reminds them that we love them and want to connect with them—and that Jesus loves them and desires that connection too.

Spread Your fragrance through me, Lord, I prayed. *May it be strong, like the smell of a middle school boy's Axe body spray after gym class. But sweet, like a child's breath after eating a bag of Skittles. And welcoming, like a freshly baked apple crisp pulled from the oven on a cool autumn day.*

To Take This Deeper

Give Because He Gave

- **Reflect:** What are some ways that people in your life have been Christ's aroma to you? Who can you spread Christ's aroma to today?
- **Take Action:** Just do it, that nice thing you keep thinking about doing for someone else—a neighbor, a coworker, a friend, a relative. Just do it.
- **Read:** Read Ephesians 4:17–5:21. Find delight in spreading Christ's aroma while you live as a child of light.

I'm Still Afraid of the Dark, Among Other Things

Give Me Jesus

*Our greatest fear as individuals and as a
church should not be of failure but of succeeding
at things in life that don't really matter.*

—Tim Kizziar[1]

I slept horribly last night. I woke up after a series of horrible nightmares, drenched with sweat and out of breath, my heart beating profusely. I woke up feeling afraid.

I thought I would outgrow this kind of fear, the kind where I am afraid of the dark and feel paranoid of bad guys who could be lurking around the corner. The kind where I have to take a deep breath before I make the ten-step run through the blackness between our bed and the toilet for my midnight pee. But I have always been afraid of the dark.

My big brother was good at exploiting my weakness. We

both slept in the basement growing up. At bedtime he would sprint downstairs to turn off all the lights and hide. The moment he jumped out and shouted, I would throw myself to the floor, lie flat on my back, kick my legs in the air like a cockroach, and scream. We nicknamed this pose "Self-Defense Mode." Although "Complete and Absolute Surrender" might be more accurate.

Husband and I discovered our own version of Self-Defense Mode one of the first nights we slept in our new apartment. It was one o'clock in the morning. We were peacefully sleeping, happy to be in our new home, until we were startled awake by the sound of shattering glass in the kitchen. In the fog of sleep and in the terror of hearing shattering glass, my mind jumped to the worst-case scenario: *We are going to DIE.*

All of the warnings we were given before choosing to live near Chicago flooded my mind: *Oh my goodness gracious, they were right! All this city has to offer are guns and high taxes!*

After what felt like hours of paralyzing fear, Husband and I finally got the guts to slink out of bed and peek outside our bedroom door. We didn't see any movement, didn't hear anyone stepping on the glass that must be covering the floor, so we courageously walked out into the kitchen to investigate what had happened.

A framed picture had fallen off the wall. *You have got to be kidding me.*

We swept and vacuumed the glass as best we could. We double-checked that the doors were locked and that no bad guys were hiding in any dark corners, nooks, or crannies. We got back into bed. We stared at each other, wide-awake and horribly freaked out. I swear my heart was still beating 536 times per minute. I thought about getting another swab of deodorant for how much I was nervously sweating but then remembered it would require that ten-step run through the blackness from our bed to the bathroom.

We finally calmed ourselves down and settled in for sleep. And then we heard the *absolute same* unnerving sound of shattering glass in the kitchen. This time we were sure somebody was out there, robbing us and probably, of course, about to kill us.

Husband stood by the bedroom door and yelled out into the kitchen. He yelled things I am not allowed to share due to the oath I swore to protect his manhood, but let me say that the words yelled by my knight in shining armor would have driven any predator out of our apartment, down the stairs, and probably to the church across the street.

If there had been an actual predator in our home. Another picture frame had fallen off the wall.

This is the part where I tell you that this chapter isn't actually about fear but about how you should *never* buy those sticky wall hooks to hang up heavy picture frames in your home instead of using a hammer and nails. It doesn't matter if you don't own the apartment you're living in and will eventually have to putty and paint the walls.

Those hooks are not worth the anxiety you will experience when your picture frames fall off the walls and make the sound of shattering glass in the middle of the night. Twice. And all God's people said, "Amen."

I joke about my fear of the dark, but there are other fears that aren't quite so funny to me, fears that have taken time to let go of and place at the foot of the cross where Christ died in order to set me free.

Fears like when I was growing up and could list at least

fifty-six things I didn't like about my body. Like wanting to develop my writing but only judging my talent on whether a blog post had impressed other people rather than whether it reflected God's truth. Like worrying about how we will survive off one salary and fund Baby's education without having to live in a van down by the river. Like wanting to be in control of what will happen and when it will happen rather than being willing to pray, *Thy will be done, Lord.*

All kinds of fears creep in and create doubt. I worry that I am not good enough to be loved by God or used by God. I question whether God is good enough to take care of us no matter what we are facing.

Sometimes these doubts and fears make me stronger in my faith. They help me come to a more vivid understanding of how much I need to rely on God. How I am not "good enough" on my own but am still so deeply loved and still able to be used by Him anyway. Other times these doubts threaten to unravel my faith. They pull me away from God's perfect love and hold me back from living up to His potential within me, from experiencing His big grace and big love the way they were meant to be enjoyed.

Fear, like any emotion, can be a natural response to my circumstances. But fear, like any emotion, should not control my decisions or actions. Because that is where faith comes in. Faith is what I choose to believe and what I choose to do *in spite* of the fear that I feel. Faith is the anchor in the storms of life's circumstances and emotions. While fear might try to keep me from doing the good work God prepared for me to do, faith keeps me moving forward, even if just one shaky baby step at a time.

In this broken and scary world it is natural to feel afraid

at times, but I should never let fear control me, never let it keep me from following God where He is leading. I shouldn't forget how my fear can be interrupted with Scripture and all of its strengthening promises.

As 1 John speaks to me: "Perfect love drives out fear" (4:18).

As Psalm 56 reminds me: "When I am afraid, I put my trust in you. In God, whose word I praise—in God I trust and am not afraid" (vv. 3–4).

As Hebrews 13 comforts me: "The Lord is my helper; I will not be afraid" (v. 6).

This is where *giving* is so important. I need to *give up*, let go, cast away, lift in prayer all my fears to the Lord. Even in the darkest of nights I need to cry out, "Give me Jesus!" and hold on to the One whose perfect love drives out fear, the One who is trustworthy, the One who helps. Sometimes I can't even try to grip or cling or hold on but instead have to let myself be held in His capable hands. It's not about finding more will-power or relying on myself to do better. It's about calling on Jesus for His power to overcome my fears and relying on His power to give me courage to move forward or to stop moving, courage to say yes or no, courage to do what I am supposed to do in spite of what I feel afraid of.

So I talk to myself. I ask myself a lot of questions: *What fears hold you back, Self? Fears related to self-consciousness? Ridicule? Failure? Guilt? Pride? For whatever has happened in your life to make you feel afraid, to make you harbor those fears, I am so sorry, Self. I pray God will reveal His comfort to you, as well as the freedom to let go and continue on in faith despite those fears. I pray He will eventually—even slowly if necessary—change your emotion of fear to peace, your doubt to an understanding of His great love for you.*

I pray I will not let my fears, my emotions, or my worldly desires get in the way of recognizing what is truly worth clinging to—that is, Christ. I'm not talking about a naïve fearlessness where I think nothing bad is ever going to happen to me. But I'm talking about a trusting fearlessness that the God I serve will carry me through anything we come to, even if my worst nightmares become my reality.

In *Holding On to Hope*, a book about the loss of two of her children and her grief thereafter, Nancy Guthrie shared,

> [My husband] says he has always feared a tragedy in his life. But he says that now that the tragedy has come, the fear is gone. Now that he has experienced his greatest fear, and experienced God's supreme faithfulness to us through this difficulty, he no longer fears tragedy in our lives. We know God more fully because we've experienced Him more fully through our sorrow.[2]

I may fear I have a lot to lose if I don't get everything I hope to gain in this world, but like the apostle Paul, am I able to say everything is rubbish compared to knowing Christ? Am I able to lay it all before the cross and put my faith in Christ and my love for Him before everything else?

With all the ways I get wrapped up in this world, I might be afraid of the direction God leads at times. I may fear I have too much to lose based on my insecurities and trials in the past. However, if I don't give up my fear and instead give up my faith, if I ignore Christ's direction in my life, or if I choose to throw myself to the ground in Self-Defense Mode, there is so much more to lose.

To Take This Deeper

Give Me Jesus

- **Reflect:** What are you afraid of? Is there something in your life you are afraid of losing or missing out on if you choose to give generously? How are your fears holding you back from giving?
- **Take Action:** Lay it all before the Lord. Understand that laying down your fears and casting your cares on God is necessary to do each day. Sometimes it is a daily struggle to let go and trust where God is leading you. And while you place your fears into God's hands, take steps to live in faith in spite of your fears.
- **Read:** Read Ephesians 6:10–20. Arm yourself in the Lord's mighty power, and "fearlessly make known the mystery of the gospel, for which [you are] an ambassador" (vv. 19–20).

Thirteen

Starved World

Give Anyway

Considering who we are in light of a holy and just
God, the only thing we truly deserve is hell. . . . If
God never does anything more than redeem us,
He has already done far more than we deserve.

—Joe Stowell, *Our Daily Bread*[1]

Last Saturday it was forty-degrees-and-the-flu-waiting-to-happen outside. Today it was sixty degrees and sunny. Simply lovely, so we made a second attempt to go to Starved Rock State Park.

But the place was packed, which meant these were our two parking options: Park a quadrillion miles away and forge through the wilderness to get to the welcome center. Or draw straws to see which of us would break the other's leg, and take one of the open handicap parking spots right up front. (Husband said no.)

On our long walk toward the welcome center, we heard

people shouting. Two cars were stopped, and the drivers were out of their vehicles, yelling at each other over an empty parking space they both wanted.

It turned out that the driver of the first car, Car #1, had passed this specific parking spot because it was full. But as soon as he passed it, the parked car backed out, leaving that spot open. The driver of Car #1 tried to back up and take the spot. He should have kept driving forward and looked for a new place to park. He should have let the driver of Car #2, who was next in line and should get this parking spot due to the Natural Order of Things, take it. But he didn't.

And Car #2's driver was angry about it. So he yelled and honked his horn and got out of his car and demanded parking-lot justice: "It's *your* fault! These people are backed up and waiting for *you*!"

By then there were at least ten vehicles stuck behind them. Multiple people were yelling, lots of horns were honking, and no cars were moving. The entire parking lot at Starved Rock State Park came to an impasse. Over a parking spot. Simply lovely.

The driver of Car #2 deserved something he wasn't getting, and we all know in the United States of America that if somebody thinks he deserves something, he is going to raise a stink. Even if it's over something as trivial as a parking spot. *Especially* if it's over something as trivial as a parking spot.

I mentioned before how I feel about the word *deserve*.

According to the world we live in, it makes the most sense to look after yourself and fight for what you *deserve*. But what if the man from Car #2 got back in his car, drove past the parking spot he deserved to find a new one, and walked a farther distance to the welcome center on his completely capable legs instead? What if he worried less about what he deserved and considered more what he could selflessly give? What if?

I know it doesn't make sense to give in these ways, not in a situation like this where somebody "deserved" something. But what if we gave in ways that didn't make sense anyway?

I will never forget the night Husband and I celebrated Guatemala's Independence Day our first year living there. We were with a group of eight gringo friends from work, soaking up all the cultural parades, marching bands, fireworks, city fairs, and street food. And then our group made its way on foot to a concert. We all cut through streets that were usually a bustling market of fruits, vegetables, and people during the day but were now an eerily quiet, trash-laden stretch of road by night.

In the distance we saw three young men beneath a street-light. Walking closer, we realized they were beating and kicking another young man lying on the ground. Husband and I had been in Guatemala for only a month and a half, but I think watching a beating happen before our very eyes conjured the same emotions of fear and confliction it would in any country. All ten of us stopped and nervously debated with each other:

"What should we do?"

"There are only three of them and ten of us."

"But one of them could have a knife or a gun!"

"And we don't know why they are beating him."

"Maybe he stole something."

"Maybe he is in the wrong gang and is walking the wrong streets tonight."

"Maybe he is completely innocent."

"Does it matter? They are beating him!"

All ten of us walked away. We did the sensible thing and chose to walk away, to look away. And I hate myself for it.

I know it wouldn't have made sense for me, a tall gringa, to run over and try to stop a fight between four young men who spoke a different language, when I didn't understand the situation or the reasons they were beating him. It would have been reckless to put my own safety and well-being at risk for whatever this young man did or didn't do. I deserved safety. I didn't deserve cuts or bruises or injuries for something I wasn't involved in.

But, oh, how I wish I had given anyway. How I wish I had done what didn't make any sense. How I wish I had run over there without thinking for so long about what I deserved and thrown my body over that young man's in order to protect him from another blast of pain to his ribs.

I don't know what would have happened. Maybe the beating would have stopped; maybe it wouldn't have. I'll never know. But what if I chose to give anyway, even when it didn't make sense? What if I chose to listen to Jesus speak into my heart, *I gave anyway.*

He didn't make sense either. He gave up heavenly glory. He hung out with society's scumbags. He dissed society's elite. He washed His disciples' stinky feet, healed the sick on the Sabbath, and died as a perfect man for imperfect people. He, least of all, "deserved" the punishment, the torture, and the death He endured.

But I gave anyway.

We live in a starved world full of starved people hungry for Christ's selfless kind of love that doesn't make any sense. But I'm too busy doing all the stuff that makes sense: striving for a comfortable job with a comfortable paycheck that can afford a comfortable home and a comfortable retirement. All within my comfortable, five-foot-radius, personal-space bubble. I make sense to the world, and that is a scary thought. I was struck by a Bible passage the other day, mostly because of the note I wrote next to the chapter heading "An Eye for an Eye." Matthew 5:38–42 says this:

"You have heard that it was said, 'Eye for eye, and tooth for tooth.' But I tell you, do not resist an evil person. If anyone slaps you on the right cheek, turn to them the other cheek also. And if anyone wants to sue you and take your shirt, hand over your coat as well. If anyone forces you to go one mile, go with them two miles. Give to the one who asks you, and do not turn away from the one who wants to borrow from you."

Choose humility over "my rights." That's the note I wrote next to "An Eye for an Eye." I don't know where or when I wrote that note, but I can honestly say I miss opportunities to do that all the time. I usually value my rights more, because I usually want what I think I deserve, because I'm too busy protecting what I believe I'm entitled to. Like in my marriage, in my relationships, and in those moments when I encounter three men beating up another man. In those moments God whispers into my heart to forgive.

After we saw those young men assault the other one, I lost it. I cried and cried and couldn't get it together. I begged Husband to take me home and forget about the concert. Forget any more celebration.

On our walk home Husband and I talked about what we saw. We talked about how we wished we had known the right thing to do. We talked about how whether or not we had known the right thing to do, we wished we had stepped in and tried to stop the beating, tried to do *something*. We wished that beyond our intense fear we had listened to the example of Christ that said, *It didn't make any sense, but I gave anyway.*

While walking home, we got stuck in the crowds as one of many marching bands paraded by. In all the commotion, a man who was quite obviously poor and quite obviously drunk stumbled and fell in the streets. In just a few seconds, he would be trampled by the marching band, whose big costumes and oversize instruments blocked their view of the road directly in front of them.

We stopped walking. This time, without taking any time to think, Husband forced his way through the crowd to help the man, stumbling drunk, back to the side of the road to safety. It didn't make any sense for him to do that. Not in this starved and selfish world that we live in.

But he did it anyway.

To Take This Deeper

Give Anyway

- **Reflect:** What if you gave in ways that didn't make sense to the rest of the selfish world we live in? Have there been times when you were too stubborn to give up "your rights" when a situation called for you to be humble?
- **Take Action:** The next time you have a choice between humility and your rights, between giving

selflessly and protecting what you deserve, take a deep breath, say a prayer for guidance, and choose wisely.

- **Read:** Read Luke 10:25–37. "Go and do likewise" (v. 37). Give anyway.

My Affair with List Making

Give It a Rest

> "I don't need very much now," said the boy. "Just
> a quiet place to sit and rest. I am very tired."
> "Well," said the tree, straightening herself up as
> much as she could, "well, an old stump is good for
> sitting and resting. Come, Boy, sit down. Sit down
> and rest." And the boy did. And the tree was happy.
>
> —Shel Silverstein, *The Giving Tree*[1]

I have a dirty little secret.

Sunday is the day I go to church and I rest. By "rest," I mean I try to make it a day that is different from the other six days of the week.

> "Remember the Sabbath day by keeping it holy. Six days
> you shall labor and do all your work, but the seventh day is
> a sabbath to the LORD your God." (Ex. 20:8–10)

That's why. But that is not my dirty little secret, this is:

105

sometimes the act of resting is as easy for me to do as sticking a needle in my eye. My dad can vouch for this. He doesn't work just because he has to; he works because he *loves* to. And I am the fruit of his loins: organized, type A, low-spectrum OCD probably.

The best way for me to complete all the work I love to do in the most efficient way possible is to make a list of all the things I have to do each day. I love lists; I love crossing things off my list. As in, even though I don't always like Monday-morning chores, deleting the Clean/Laundry task from my Google Calendar brings me more satisfaction than a big, hot slice of Better Than Sex cake.

But every time Sunday rolls around, I have a difficult choice to make: Am I going to give it a rest and put my work down? Or am I going to have an affair with my to-do list?

The fact that Monday comes right after Sunday does not make it any easier. Monday is Clean/Laundry Day, so usually on Sunday my Shoulder Devil starts hissing in my ear, "You know, it would be really great to get a head start on that big Monday to-do list of yours. Laundry, scrub the bathroom, vacuum. Pluck your eyebrows too—you have a Frida Kahlo thing going on right now. Just get it all done today so you can cross it off your list. You can always rest tomorrow."

And then I get the strong itch to clean the past six days' worth of infestation in our apartment. I look like an addict going through withdrawal, nervously pacing the hallway, eyes twitching, inspecting crumbs on the kitchen floor and body hairs on the bathroom floor. Pretty much dying to get a fix of all-purpose cleaner and paper towels.

My child, you are worried and upset about many things, but only one thing is needed.

My struggle to slow down and make meaningful connections with the Lord is not rooted in some sort of personality flaw. But just as I can use being introverted as an excuse to avoid social interaction, I can use being task-oriented as an excuse for never taking the rest God designed as a gift for our busy souls. God created a day of rest for a reason. God demonstrated taking a day of rest for a reason. And my to-do-list affairs on my day of rest are a problem for a few reasons:

Rest rejuvenates me. I am a wife, mom, friend, church member, and neighbor. But if I never give myself a break from my tasks or relationship building or the other things I do in a week's time, my wires will eventually go on the fritz. Maybe not after one week; maybe not even after two. But eventually it will happen, because ours is a culture of worker's burnout. (There has to be a better way! A better way to recognize our limits and incorporate rest into our weekly lives! Oh yeah, it's called the Sabbath.)

> Return to your rest, my soul,
>> for the LORD has been good to you. (Ps. 116:7)

Rest reminds me that success is not related to accomplishments. I know that it is a good thing to find pleasure in the work that I do. However, my value is not found in what I do but in who I am as a child of the Father. I am His daughter, one whom He cherishes and desires to come to Him when she is weary. Taking time to rest and be with Him is a successful day indeed.

> "Come to me, all you who are weary and burdened, and I will give you rest." (Matt. 11:28)

Rest is more than taking a nap. Don't get me wrong; sometimes a nap is exactly the sacred rest I need in this stage of life—taking care of a small person on too few hours of sleep. But there are other times when "be still, and know that I am God" (Ps. 46:10) calls for something other than subconscious activity. And I honestly don't like to simply "be still," no distractions, no music, no nothing. You want me to go to church? *Yes!* You want me to take a nap? *Absolutely!* You want me to sit and read a few chapters of my Bible? *Great! I'll cross it off my list when I'm done!* But you want me to simply sit and be still? You want me to take quiet time for prayer and listening? *You people are crazy!* But in a world where we can't even handle watching TV without being on our phones, too, this kind of rest is healing. As difficult to do as sticking a needle in my eye, but necessary.

> Yes, my soul, find rest in God;
> my hope comes from him. (Ps. 62:5)

Rest demonstrates a wholesome life. Just as our neighbors—both in and out of the church—need to see us sharing Christ's love and sacrifice with them, they also need to see us living real, healthy, and whole lives that don't lead to burnout. Darren Prince wrote,

> *When ministry is your life*, you will give when you have nothing to give, work when you should be resting, neglect that which should be your greatest priority, and ultimately loathe the very people you are called to love. . . . On the other hand, *when your life is your ministry*, all of life becomes a sacrament before God: your work and your

rest, your eating and sleeping, your generosity and your neediness, your care for your body and the environment, your trivial pastimes and your greatest accomplishments.[2]

I know Sunday or Sabbath-day activities could be heavily debated. This day of rest was designed as a gift to God's people, not meant to become a legalistic law (Mark 2:23–28). But for me, a big way to make Sunday different from the other six days is to just put down the all-purpose cleaner and slowly walk away. A big way the Lord says "I love you" is when He reminds me of the gift that is found in His rest.

My child, you are worried and upset about many things, but only one thing is needed. Stop, sit at My feet, and listen to what I have to say.

This whole to-do-list-affair thing takes me back to the kitchen of Mary and Martha, two sisters who welcomed Jesus into their home (Luke 10:38–42). One sister, Mary, recognized the opportunity to spend time with Jesus. The other sister, my homegirl Martha, struggled to give it a rest. I once wrote a personal interpretation of the story in a blog post:

While Jesus was traveling with His disciples, sisters Mary and Martha opened their home to Him. When He arrived, Mary stopped what she was doing, sat at Christ's feet, and listened to what He had to say.

Martha freaked out.

She was "distracted by all the preparations that had to be made." She had a to-do list. She was a "work before play" kind of girl. If she could just get all the cooking and cleaning and preparations finished, then she might be able to sit with her guest. She even asked Jesus to scold Mary for her. "Lord, don't You care that my sister left me to do the work by myself? Tell her to help me!"

I am a Martha. I am a "work before play . . . or die" kind of girl. I am a head down, charging through the day, trying to get everything done on my to-do list that never ends. I am usually charging so fast that I often don't recognize the people or the opportunities I am charging by. I'd rather be crossing something off my list.

"Martha, Martha," the Lord answered. "You are worried and upset about many things, but only one thing is needed. Mary has chosen what is better, and it will not be taken away from her."

Mary knew. Mary recognized the opportunity in front of her, the amazing opportunity to simply sit at Jesus' feet and listen to the words He said. Nothing else mattered. All her work, duties, and surrounding circumstances were properly put on the back burner as she sat at her Savior's feet in precious fellowship with Him.

Jesus knew too. He knew that Martha needed a break. He knew that she needed to stop what she was doing, rest with Him, and listen to His words of life. He knows that we still need that today.

Do I recognize my opportunities each day? The precious opportunities to stop, sit at Christ's feet, and simply listen to what He is trying to say to me? No, not often enough.

Kendra, Kendra. You are distracted by all the preparations you think you have to make.

Shower, work, clean, wash, dry, e-mail, errands, sweep, cook, rinse, tidy, collapse. Repeat.

Kendra, Kendra. You are worried and upset about many things, but only one thing is needed.
Stop, sit at My feet, and listen to what I have to say.[3]

This world needs both Marys and Marthas. But as a Martha, I have this one big thing I can learn from my sister Mary, no matter how annoyed I am at the fact she isn't pulling her weight in the kitchen: sometimes I need to just stop buzzing around for a minute. Sometimes I just need to rest. Even if it's as hard as sticking a needle in my eye.

My child, you are worried and upset about many things, but only one thing is needed. Stop, sit at My feet, and listen to what I have to say.

To Take This Deeper

Give It a Rest

- **Reflect:** In what ways do you give it a rest on your Sunday or Sabbath day? Do you recognize when you need to give it a rest, or are you more prone to push yourself to burnout? Remember that while some seasons in life are busier than others, a weekly day of rest is one thing that should stay constant. Not as an annoying rule but as a blessing to our rushed hearts and minds.
- **Take Action:** It's Day 14. Find time to give it a rest at Jesus' feet. Find a quiet space to be still and pray and listen.

- **Read:** Read Genesis 1:1–2:3. Take in both God's amazing acts of wonder and His first demonstration of giving it a rest.

Fifteen

One Quarter Short
of a Laundry Load

Give Us Our Daily Bread

*Truth is, I think, if God just gave us our
daily bread, many of us would be angry.*

—Francis Chan[1]

This afternoon I was one quarter short of a laundry load.

I have been called worse things in my life, but being one quarter short of a laundry load meant that my mountain of Monday laundry was going to have a hard time getting done—or at least a hard time getting dried. I needed $3.50 worth of quarters to wash two loads and dry one extra-large load, but I was stuck at $3.25.

I had options. I could ask one of our neighbors for a quarter in exchange for two dimes and a nickel. I could wait until Husband got home in a few hours and take our car to the bank. Or I could use our chairs, curtain rods, hangers, bedposts, and couch to hang up all our wet clothes to dry. But none of those sounded like a great option. A "great option" would have been making sure I had enough quarters earlier than the exact moment I wanted to do laundry.

I started the two loads of wash anyway. The machines took thirty-seven minutes to cycle, which meant I had roughly thirty-seven minutes to figure out where my last quarter was going to come from.

I was stuck at one of life's greatest crossroads. One part of me wanted to take a left and go ask a neighbor for a quarter so that I wouldn't be forced to leave my work tasks for later. And the other part of me would rather just turn around, shut the door, and forget I ever had such a horrifying idea. My inner Type A Workhorse was battling my inner Introvert. Classic Jekyll and Hyde.

After minutes of inner turmoil, I decided to just go for it. I would brave up enough to ask a neighbor for a quarter in exchange for two dimes and a nickel, and I would humble myself enough to get over the fact that I was asking for something we should have already provided for ourselves.

The problem was that most people in our apartment building were gone at work. Most except Joan. I thought I would ask her first. I hadn't seen her recently, which meant she hadn't been able to see Baby run circles around her either. With thirty-three minutes until dry time, I knocked on her door. Baby knocked too.

Knock, knock, knock. No answer. Darn.

We went back upstairs to our apartment. We played while I counted down the rest of the minutes until the laundry machines were done. And I got slightly annoyed because time was passing and a quarter wasn't magically appearing in my pocket.

"Give us this day our daily bread."

That verse—Matthew 6:11 (NKJV)—hung on our prayer wall, and now it was staring me down, scolding my attitude. Not because I was supposed to drop down on my knees and pray for a quarter, but because God already had provided my daily bread. He already had provided the vehicle, gas, and cash to exchange bills at the bank this afternoon. He already had provided the chairs, curtain rods, hangers, bedposts, and couch to hang our clothes on to dry if that's what this came down to.

Yes, I already gave you this day your daily bread.

I did not actually need a quarter. My life and breath did not depend on it. But it's a lifelong lesson to me, having grown up in suburbia, that my daily bread is usually a lot less than I think. As Francis Chan preached:

> Truth is, I think, if God just gave us our daily bread, many of us would be angry. "That's all you're going to give me? You're just going to give me enough to sustain me for today? What about tomorrow or next year or 10, 20, 30 years from now? I want to know that I'm set up." And yet Jesus says just pray for your daily provisions.[2]

I often carelessly pray that prayer, expecting a lot more than what I need to survive one day at a time, even one moment at a time.

How humbling to actually pray, *Give us this day our daily bread.* How humbling to remember that everything I need—and receive beyond my needs—comes from God's hands.

How humbling to take the perspective of *Wow, Lord, You have given us so much* compared to *Lord, it's only a quarter. Seriously?!* How humbling to gratefully accept whatever God provides as my daily bread, however He provides, through whomever He provides.

My #FirstWorldProblems that morning made me think of our friends Pablino and Victoria. They lived on the other side of the fence from the school we worked at in Guatemala. At times we would go through the gate and make our way down a skinny dirt path to visit them. It was like walking into a completely different world. Corn stood seven feet high. Children ran around in grimy, mismatched clothes. Homes, including theirs, were made of tin and cardboard slapped together over a dirt floor. There was an open-door policy for dogs, chickens, and flies. All the third-world stereotypes were prevalent.

But it was there, in that completely different world, where we got to know Guatemala a little better, where we got to meet two faces and perspectives we didn't encounter every day inside our classrooms and fences. Our eyes were opened; our minds were stretched. Our hearts were softened.

Most of our visits began by listening to the latest ailments of Pablino's aged and tired body. Sometimes we weren't even sitting down on our plastic stools yet before his tears began to flow as he described more of the endless physical pain he was suffering. We asked friends and family in the States to donate money to pay for Pablino's medicine, so each time we visited we dropped off enough for that month's supply.

When our conversation, fly swatting, and Baby snuggling came to an end on one particular visit, Victoria handed me two little eggs from their chicken, which lived with them and eight other chickens in their one-room shack. Out of their intense poverty, their sickness, and their struggle, they gave us two little eggs. It was her way of saying thank you for the money we delivered each month.

At first, it was hard to accept. Their chickens were meant to feed them, not us. Not two healthy gringos whose supply of daily bread was more than enough. But the genuine smile on Victoria's face as she placed those two smooth eggs in my hand told me it was the absolute right thing to do. To receive and remember all that two little eggs can teach you, all that two little eggs can breathe into your heart.

See how I gave you this day your daily bread through this gesture, through these friends, through this time of visiting together. See how I provided just enough of what you need.

Not only did those two little eggs fill our stomachs for dinner that evening, but they still remind me over and over that the answer to "Give us this day our daily bread" is usually a lot less than I think. That the other half of humbly praying, *Lord, please give us this day our daily bread*, is the humble act of accepting whatever He provides, however He provides, through whomever He provides it. Those two little eggs remind me what a precious gift it is when the body of Christ supports one another, prays for one another, and shares our daily bread with one another, from all different sides of all different kinds of fences.

After the thirty-seven minutes of the washing cycle passed, plus an extra forty-five more minutes in which I was caught upstairs taking care of Baby, I knew the laundry machines were done cycling. And after a quick glance outside, I knew that our neighbors Josh and Christina were home from work too.

Josh and Christina were the first neighbors we were really able to connect with beyond "Hi, how are you?" and, "Good, you?" It could be their nice faces that make you feel comfortable when you meet for the first time. It could be that they're the kind of people you want to spend a random Friday night with drinking wine, eating handfuls of M&M's, and binge watching funny YouTube videos. It could be that they wouldn't even take my two dimes and nickel when I knocked on their door and asked for a quarter.

Christina brought out her wallet bursting with quarters and said they were happy to share. "We just replenished our stock," she told me with a big smile.

Sometimes God gives us exactly our daily bread. Sometimes He provides more. And sometimes our own cups overflow in abundance. Sometimes God gives us our daily bread in a convenient fashion. Sometimes He provides it through hard work and sweat and tears. And sometimes everything about it feels inconvenient.

But God provides. Whether it's two little eggs from our impoverished friends in Guatemala or a quarter from our neighbors to dry our laundry, it all comes from Him.

To Take This Deeper

Give Us Our Daily Bread

- **Reflect:** In what ways does God provide what you need, when you need it, one day at a time? How has God used other people to provide what you need? Remember that asking God for our daily bread means humbly opening our hands to *whatever*, *however*, and *through whomever* He provides it.

- **Take Action:** Are you in a place of great need in your life? Humbly ask God to provide exactly what you need one day at a time. Are you in a place of great abundance in your life? Humbly ask God to show you how you can share that abundance of daily bread with others.

- **Read:** Read 2 Corinthians 8:1–15. Be inspired by the Macedonian churches, who, in great poverty, overflowed with rich generosity. They gave beyond what they needed for their daily bread.

Sixteen

Your Breath Smells Like Gospel

Give a Call

*Your life will be richer for forging a
relationship with friends so committed
to you they will not tolerate your getting
away with sweeping dirt under the rug.*

—Michael W. Smith, *Friends Are Friends Forever*[1]

I don't think friendships need to be labeled with cute words like *best* or *forever* when you become a grown-up. But using words like *influential* and *spiritually formative* sound a little sixth-century monk, if you ask me.

Forever friends can be the kind that naturally ebb and flow and last as you make your way through different stages of life. Sometimes they show up at just the right time or become like family away from family. Other times forever friends are the kind where you reach such a divine level of comfort that you'd even hug them without a bra on. Or at least say out loud, "I'd hug you, but I forgot to put a bra on."

I've had the kind of friendship that has lasted nearly my whole life, since that blessed time in the nineties when we traded "Best Friends" necklaces with each other and wrote down our secret language with gel pens. We stuck it out through the awkward years when we thought it was hilarious to do stuff like sing in public for people's spare change and make embarrassing videos of ourselves lip-syncing to the *Space Jam* soundtrack. They're the kind of friends who understand exactly where I come from.

I've had the kind of friendship that showed up at just the right time, like the friend who found me in high school and didn't mock those ugly bangs I thought were a good idea at the time. She sweated with me through volleyball state runners-up and state champions and then later got ready with me for the prom. She stayed close through the breakup that I swore might kill me, and she eventually stood up next to me on my wedding day.

And as someone who has lived too far away to go to Sunday dinner at Dad and Mom's since I was eighteen years old, I've also had the kind of friendship where people become like family away from family. Like that friend who came over to eat pancakes for dinner all through college. And those friends who shared experiences in foreign places, including releasing baby sea turtles into the Pacific Ocean and facing poverty every day we walked out our front doors. And like those friends who guided me through my first pregnancy and year of motherhood in a different country. All like a precious lifeline.

No, not all friendships are like this, nor do they have to be. Not all friendships are influential or spiritually formative or lasting, but how I treasure the ones that become deep. The kind where, past the conversations and commonalities and laughter, you go through some of the really hard stuff that makes most others shy away. You feel comfortable welcoming them beyond the outside crust of your life to your inner soul. And no matter what you are thinking or feeling or doing, they will handle you with loving care, and you will just as quickly do the same for them. The kind that stand close enough to whisper God's "I love yous" into your soul, and you could easily say back, "Your breath smells like gospel." These are the kind of friendships that make life richer, deeper, and better.

> If either of them falls down,
>> one can help the other up.
> But pity anyone who falls
>> and has no one to help them up. (Eccl. 4:10)

I'm learning that sometimes it's hard to be an adult and a friend at the same time. No longer do I have the open weekends of a high schooler or the energy of a toddler. I don't live within play-date distance from all the people I'd love to keep close contact with. The background music of our lives isn't exactly the carefree sounds of Black Eyed Peas and Usher anymore. And that's cool; I still think we're pretty cool. It just takes a little more effort to intentionally connect as life takes us down different paths.

But even as infrequent as those intentional connections might be, I love how meaningful those connections have become. What a blessing it is to watch forever friends grow as spouses, parents, and talented people. To walk each other through our messes, pains, and heartaches. To celebrate each other through our accomplishments, milestones, and greatest joys. Even if it's weeks or months or a year without much catch-up, I love getting the text from my friend celebrating that her kid went an entire day without peeing all over herself. Or an e-mailed blog post that made her cry ugly, black-mascara tears. Or the phone call that simply says, "I miss you."

Which is why I was so grateful to intentionally connect with one of my forever friends that Tuesday. Kaylee is her name, and she is that friend who found me in high school and now lives too many hours away. We video chatted for an hour and a half that afternoon, both of us with babies crawling all over us, pulling our hair, and totally butting in to the conversation. But it was precious, like a sappy tribute to the bounty of life we have been blessed to walk through with each other. (I could almost hear Michael W. Smith softly yet powerfully singing "Friends are friends forever" in the background.)

It had been at least a month since Kaylee and I had last talked, but she has this way of coming around at just the right time—like that day. I knew our move back to the States from Guatemala would be a difficult transition and that looking for a new congregation and new friends would be exhausting. I knew that parenting a child would never get easier and that embarking on this journey of praying and seeking and writing would be challenging. But it had all accumulated to a lot of anxiety and fear, a knot of apprehension sitting on my chest that didn't seem to want to pack its bags and leave.

And that's where friendship with a person like Kaylee is such a gift. Even just one forever friend can provide great stability, love, truth, and some of the Lord's reassurance when my heart feels like it has been ransacked by life's weary load. I need someone who will intentionally connect and listen and ask questions and say things like,

"Yes, I agree. There are times when parenting makes me so frustrated."

"Yes, I also struggle with what it means to 'remember the Sabbath day and keep it holy.'"

"Yes, I have also been working on my prayer life lately. Is there any way I can pray for you today?"

I crave this kind of commitment, honesty, and compassion—the things that get wrapped up in our favorite church buzzword called *community*. I crave the gift of being in the relationships that breathe the gospel into each other's lives, relationships where we know each other's weaknesses and vulnerabilities, relationships where we see each other screw up and choose to love each other anyway.

What a gift to find that in a friend, whether that person has been in your life through its entirety or only for a short time. It's such a blessing to find a friend who is able to say, "I love you no matter what, and also let me note how you're being kind of an idiot right now" or "You're going through a tough time? Let me drive three hours to visit you for the day." It's a treasure to find a friend who makes you pee a little when you laugh, or hugs you through the ugly, black-mascara tears, even when she forgot to wear a bra. And how rich to know you'd do the same for her in return. It's so beautiful to recognize that God made us for Himself but also for each other.

Be devoted to one another in love. Honor one another above yourselves. (Rom. 12:10)

I wish there was a simple formula to concoct these kinds of friendships, one that I could use to make new friends in our new city. But unlike shoving our bodies into a strong pair of Spanx, some things in life simply can't be forced, only prayed and searched for. And I *am* praying for it: friendship that's like a fresh breath of gospel when I need it. Friendship that might be waiting only a few yards away if we're willing to step out of our front door to first say hello, if we're willing to put in the time and effort and conversation.

I think of our neighbor Joan, who invited us into her home to let Baby run and play with her exercise ball. I think of our neighbor Jim, who bought us a Jimmy John's gift card to welcome us to our apartment building, and the warm apple crisp I made and that Husband shared with Jim on a cool autumn day. I think of our neighbors Josh and Christina, who shared a quarter with me so that I could finish doing the laundry. What a gift; what a delightful gift.

> How good and pleasant it is
>> when God's people live together in unity! (Ps. 133:1)

After living a few years here and a couple of years there, I've found it's exhausting meeting new people. It's draining—for extroverts and introverts alike—getting past the initial stages of hello with a stranger, or putting in the time and effort and conversation to reach the "Hey, I think we're friends" stage. But I've also found it's worth the prayer and the search, because I never know when one of those friendships might become influential, spiritually formative, maybe even lasting—and might lead to making life richer, deeper, and better than it was before.

> A friend loves at all times,
>> and a brother is born for a time of adversity. (Prov. 17:17)

Today God's "I love you" came through one of my forever friends to tell me, to show me:

Life isn't always easy, but keep at it.

I'm praying for you.

I care enough about you to call and spend time with you.

You are special.

You are loved.

You are worth investing my time.

You are my friend.

Her breath smelled just like gospel. And I am so grateful.

To Take This Deeper

Give a Call

- **Reflect:** Who makes your life richer, deeper, and better than it was before? Are there any people in your life—new faces at church, work, or the neighborhood—you've thought about pursuing friendship with?
- **Take Action:** Pray for your forever friends or for that friendship that you are starting with someone new. And take action: make a call; write an encouraging note; plan some time to intentionally connect and breathe the gospel into each other's lives.

- **Read:** Read Philippians 1:1–11. Work to cultivate the kind of friendships that are a partnership in the gospel and that acknowledge Christ's good work in each other.

Don't Be Surprised When He Answers

Give Him a Chance

> *God will either give us what we ask or*
> *give us what we would have asked if*
> *we knew everything he knows.*
>
> —Timothy Keller, *Prayer: Experiencing*
> *Awe and Intimacy with God*[1]

Baby had this new game she loved to play.

She waddled her squishy-diapered bottom into her room, slammed the door, and then rapped on it as though she were trying to escape from prison. My indispensable role in this game was to open the door.

And then her face. When she saw me on the other side, her face lit up like a Christmas tree: shock and awe and pure delight. Her face said, *Oh my goodness gracious! I didn't know you were standing right there on the other side of the door,*

Mommy! I didn't know you were going to answer! It is so great to see you! And the door is open! Let freedom ring!

And then she slammed the door in my face again.

Sometimes Baby would mix it up. Sometimes she would also ceremoniously hand me a little toy and then two seconds later demand I return the toy like the generous Toddler she was most likely becoming. And then she would slam the door in my face. Again.

We played this game over and over and over. Over and over and over to the point where if someone asked me what I did today, my cheeks might turn pink and I might start stammering to come up with a socially acceptable answer.

And can I be honest for two secs? While I was brimming with love for my child and her enthusiasm for one thousand repetitions of this game, I was *bored out of my brains.* We were on the third day of being at home by ourselves. Day three with no car and a dark autumn sky that gloomed at us and said, "I'm sorry. You won't be leaving your two-bedroom-one-bathroom apartment today." This homebody really could have used some company. I really could have used some conversation to fish my Mom Brain out of the toy box for a while. I needed a change, needed a face, needed an adult.

But even here God speaks. If I'm paying attention, even here in these mundane, ordinary moments when I am *bored out of my brains,* I will feel His quiet "I love yous" stirring deep in my soul. Because as Baby played this little game over and over, I was reminded that this was a lot like a game I like to play: a game called My Prayer Life.

I impatiently rap on heaven's door. I read off my list of needs to the Lord like I'm ordering fast food at a drive-through. (*Yes, Lord, I would like fries with that.*) If I'm feeling really generous, I'll add that prayer request my sister mentioned the other day. And sometimes, with the hope that the Lord will get my order right, I'll offer up my ten-dollar-bill heart full of fancy promises to be a better person as collateral. (*For real this time, Lord!*)

I thought about the past couple weeks in particular. I had stood at the door and knocked. I had prayed for a lot of things. But sometimes I still had a hard time believing God is really standing on the other side of heaven's door. Sometimes I still felt surprised when God opened the door and answered. And sometimes I offered up my heart to God and asked Him to let me be a part of His work with all my best intentions and then *still* demanded it back when I got scared, doubtful, or impatient. Like yelling, "Never mind!" and pulling the door closed in His face. Again.

I wondered why God is so patient with me. I wondered why He lets me do this over and over, why He doesn't just get out His lightning bolts now and smite me off His threshold the next time I play this feeble game with Him. I wondered why I can't seem to grasp the fact that when I pray, God listens, that He wants to hear from me and talk with me so that I can experience both awe and intimacy with Him.

Maybe instead of focusing so much on myself and my own striving and my own shortcomings, I need to simply focus more on *who* exactly it is I am praying to:

I pray to a God who is alive (Rev. 1:18).

I pray to a God who answers prayer (1 John 5:14–15).

I pray to a God who loves me as a father loves his child (Ps. 103:13).

I pray to a God who cares about the details of my life (Luke 12:22–24).

And I pray to a God who is so much bigger than all that too. God works beyond what I'm able to see through my narrow vision that gets so easily absorbed in my own life. God draws me out to understand that He's not working in just me, loving just me, caring for just me. While our relationship is personal, right down to Him knowing the very number of hairs on my head, His work, love, and care are global. God's redemptive story has been in action since before creation and spans all of creation. God is behind and beyond it all.

That is who I pray to. All that and more, much grander than my understanding.

I was struck by the story in Matthew 8 about the centurion, an officer in the Roman army. He went to Jesus and asked Him to heal his servant, and Jesus offered to go to his house and do so. But the centurion said, "Lord, I do not deserve to have you come under my roof. But just say the word, and my servant will be healed" (Matt. 8:8).

The centurion didn't demand Jesus heal his servant. He asked and then simply acknowledged Christ's authority to answer his request with healing. There was no uncertainty in his mind whether Christ could heal. There was no praying and then retraction of prayers because he doubted the ability or the timing of the God he was speaking to. And I imagine there was no shock or surprise after Christ miraculously healed the centurion's servant either. Just a whole lot of gratitude, like a simple yet highly respectful "I knew He could do it." The Bible says Jesus was astonished, that He had not met anyone in all Israel with faith like that of the centurion.

This is the kind of faith required in prayer. A humble confidence that no matter what I pray for, God answers. A childlike trust beyond all fear, doubt, and impatience that

God is able. He might not answer how I wish or in the timing I desire, but God promised long ago and still promises today that when we ask a question, seek Him out, and knock on heaven's door in prayer, He will always answer. Always open the door with welcoming arms. I should give Him the chance to do those things. Better yet, I shouldn't be surprised when He does those things.

I'm here. I'm listening. I'm waiting for you to knock. But when you knock, don't be surprised when I open the door. Don't offer up your heart and then demand it back. Trust Me.

I think it's pretty special how God speaks in the mundane and ordinary. It's pretty awesome how He's always whispering, "I love you," and it's a matter of my seeking and listening to hear it. But is it horrible to admit that even with all the special things I learned from playing Baby's game over and over and over that day, I was still *bored out of my brains*?

That was my prayer: for some company. I'd already done the nosy-neighbor thing and looked out the window to see who was home, but the parking lot was absolutely empty. Like a big sign reading, "Nobody's here! Just go back to living your lonely life!"

I'm here. I'm listening. I'm waiting for you to knock. But when you knock, don't be surprised when I open the door. Don't offer up your heart and then demand it back. Trust Me.

I shouldn't have been surprised when my phone rang. It was Tiffany, one of my beloved roommates from college in Iowa, who now lived only twenty minutes away from me on the South Side of Chicago. She called to say she was in the area and wanted to know if she could stop over and hang out for a little bit.

I *really* shouldn't have been surprised.

Are You serious, Lord? That is the kind of clear answer You are going to give my prayers today? Since when are You so obvious and quick to say yes?! I thought.

Since when are you paying close enough attention to actually notice? came the reply. #Touché.

Not only did God send a friend, but He sent one who's like a sunflower in the middle of a hayfield, like a beacon of light on those dark autumn days that just like to gloom at you. And not only did He send her at a convenient time, but He sent her on a day when my Mom Brain might have exploded in an epic way. What a sight for sore eyes.

I have stood at the door and knocked. I have asked to hear God's "I love yous." And that day I felt those whispers loud and clear:

I hear you. I will answer you. But are you listening? Are you willing to offer Me your heart and trust Me to keep it for you? To mold it? Use it in a way I know is best? Will you give Me a chance?

God answers prayers. Whether it's to know our neighbors, or to bring a dead car back to life, or to provide a friend for a lonely being, or to see the world through His eyes, He answers. Not always how I want, not always before I get impatient, but He answers.

I'm here, waiting for you to knock. But don't be surprised when I open the door. Don't be surprised when I answer.

Okay, Lord, I thought. *I will pray. I won't be surprised when You answer. And I will give thanks that, like a loving parent, You are patient with this whole knock-open-slam-the-door-in-your-face routine I like to play over and over and over.*

To Take This Deeper

Give Him a Chance

- **Reflect:** What have you prayed for recently? In what ways has God answered your prayers? Was it with a yes or a no, or a "not yet," or an "I have something different and better planned for you"? Have you given God a chance to answer, or have you already put your prayers aside?

- **Take Action:** Continue to pray for who or what is on your heart. A neighbor? A friend? Your spouse? Give God a chance to answer those prayers in His perfect timing.

- **Read:** Read Matthew 7:7–12. Ask God about what's on your heart, seek first His kingdom, and knock on heaven's door, knowing that our loving Father will open and answer.

Eighteen

"Love Ya"

Give It a Moment

*I choose to believe that there may be a thousand
big moments embedded in this day, waiting
to be discovered like tiny shards of gold.*

—Shauna Niequist, *Cold Tangerines*[1]

"Okay, I'll talk to you later. Love yaaaa . . . aaand I'll see you soon."

I knew it was a slipup. We had chatted on the phone for a while: Joan had a busy schedule of doctors' appointments. Joan's friend was in the hospital. Joan was practicing driving so she could pass her driver's test. Joan was going to her granddaughter's wedding next week. Joan was scolding me for talking to her on the phone while I drove to pick up Husband from work.

But then she slipped up. After all our chatting, Joan said, "Love ya!" Well, something more like "Love yaaaa . . . aaand I'll see you soon."

I didn't say it back. I didn't want to highlight her oopsie and make her feel uncomfortable. But I still thoroughly enjoyed hearing it. That "Love ya" still spoke volumes to my soul. Obviously that meant our conversation was comfortable enough for those words to slip out. Our conversation wasn't just some business exchange. It wasn't the doctor's office calling to order another blood test she hated so passionately. Nope, our phone conversation was between her and me: two neighbor friends. That's why she said, "Love ya" to me.

And that's why I felt so happy after our phone conversation: Joan said, "Love ya!" I am Joan's friend! Community is being built here! Right here in our apartment building! I felt all sparkly inside, like maybe we were getting past that initial stage of friendship that is so draining to get through. The iceberg of awkwardness had been broken. (*And all the introverts passed out in jubilant exhaustion.*)

Now, I realize this may highlight my special feminine skill called Reading Too Much into Something, in which I over-analyze a situation down to its threadbare underpants. I pick at all the details like an ingrown hair and then make a slightly informed and highly indecisive conclusion based on roughly 42 percent factual information. I saw this meme once: "I've got 99 problems and 86 of them are completely made up scenarios in my head that I'm stressing about for no logical reason."[2]

(But before I let men off the hook about overanalyzing things, let me say this: pregame show, game commentary, postgame show, SportsCenter.)

So, yeah, I could be Reading Too Much into Something here. Joan probably always said, "Love ya" when she talked to her many children on the phone throughout the week. Joan was at least in her eighties, and habits like saying, "Love ya" at the end of a phone conversation have a way of surviving old age. But I'm going to Read Too Much into Something anyhow. Life stays spicier that way.

And I am going to give this "Love ya," this slipup, this oopsie that I am probably just Reading Too Much into, its own honorary moment of celebration. I am going to give thanks to God for it. I'm going to let myself feel happy, because happiness isn't around all the time, and it's a good thing to embrace his bright and shiny face when he does stop by to say hello.

> The LORD is my strength and my shield;
>> my heart trusts in him, and he helps me.
> My heart leaps for joy,
>> and with my song I praise him. (Ps. 28:7)

And when I say, "Give it a moment," I don't mean I'm going to celebrate it by taking a picture and posting it on social media. That is in a separate category of celebration called Telling the World About the Yummy Sushi I Ate When Nobody Actually Cares. And I'm not going to celebrate by throwing a party, or by taking an exotic vacation to Bora-Bora, or by buying myself a fancy gift either. #Ain'tNobodyGotFundsForThat

I'm talking about an honorary moment of silence, a moment soaking up all the big feelings that I feel, a shout-out of gratitude to the God who gave me this simple yet precious gift today. I'm talking about letting all of my thoughts and feelings and praise and awe linger as long as they want to, displaying the tender love God so enjoys bestowing on His children.

There is a telling story in the Bible about when Jesus healed ten men of their leprosy (Luke 17:11–19). Leprosy, meaning these ten men were diseased, outcast, unclean, and rejected by common society. From the law-obliged safe distance, they cried out to Jesus for Him to have pity on them. But what did that mean? A scrap of food, a shroud of clothing, complete healing? They must have known who Jesus was to call Him "Master." Christ's reputation of compassion preceded Him on the roads He traveled.

But Jesus said, "Go, show yourselves to the priests" (v. 14). A seemingly strange reply, but the lepers knew that the only reason for a leper to show himself to the priests was if he had been healed. They probably stopped for a minute and looked at each other. They saw each other's scaly skin, enflamed extremities, twisted limbs, collapsed noses. Their nubs where fingers used to be. They weren't yet healed, but Jesus said, "Go."

And they did. They went; they obeyed. "And as they went, they were cleansed" (v. 14).

If the story stopped there, I could assume this was about healing as a result of faith and obedience. But that's only half the story. "One of them, when he saw he was healed, came back, praising God in a loud voice. He threw himself at Jesus' feet and thanked him—and he was a Samaritan" (vv. 15–16).

Only one of them. Only one, and he was the foreigner, the one who hadn't heard of Christ's coming salvation all the days of his life. But he was the one more sensitive to Christ's compassion, the one more touched by His mercy. All ten lepers called out "in a loud voice" for pity, but only one called out in a loud voice of praise and thanksgiving. You can feel Jesus' disappointment: "Were not all ten cleansed? Where are the other nine? Has no one returned to give praise to God except this foreigner?" (vv. 17–18).

My thoughts get haughty quickly: *Were the other nine men only going to clamor for requests, but never thank God when He answered their prayers? Did they only call on God when they needed help, but never in gratitude for the salvation they received? Where did the other nine go? Were they too busy posting pictures of their new dermatologist-approved skin on social media or planning a Welcome Back to the Village party to throw themselves to the ground at Christ's feet and thank God for what He did for them? Who does that?! Who celebrates without first saying thank you?*

So many. So many do that. And me, I do that. But then comes Scripture, once again reminding my heart:

> The LORD has done it this very day;
> let us rejoice today and be glad. (Ps. 118:24)

I'm good at celebrating the big stuff. I'm good at "giving it a moment" when I accomplish the big accomplishments I want to make, or my life is changed in the big ways I want it to be changed.

For example, when my high school volleyball team won the state title, we rode a fire truck down the street and into the school's parking lot as if it were a royal chariot of winners. And when I got engaged, my mom and I used eight whole months to plan a matrimonial event that would last a total of sixteen hours, including an honorary "wedding week" for the final seven days of preparations and decorations and pedicures. And when I got pregnant with Baby, we were given seven different baby showers to celebrate her arrival. *Seven.*

But do I say thank you before I celebrate? "Well ... um ..."

And I'm not only talking about celebrating the big stuff either. What I'm getting at by celebrating this "Love ya," this slipup, this oopsie that I am probably just Reading Too Much into, is that sometimes I forget to celebrate the small things. The baby steps. The tiny victories. The next breath of fresh oxygen. Because some of that stuff deserves a little moment in the spotlight too. Some of that stuff should conjure an attitude of thankfulness, a loud voice of praise and worship to the generous God providing it all.

Life's tough. Reading Ecclesiastes 3 quickly reminds us of that: there is a time to die, uproot, kill, tear down, weep, mourn, scatter stones, refrain from embracing, give up, throw away, tear, be silent, hate, war. But then there's the other half of that passage: there is a time to be born, plant, heal, build, laugh, dance, gather stones, embrace, search, keep, mend, speak, love, peace.

Am I celebrating these things, the precious moments that make life taste sweet like the candy Grandma always dispensed from her purse into my pudgy hands? I'm talking about that time a friend called you to remind you that she cares. And that time Grandma bought a card, wrote a note inside of it, and sent it to you in the mail. I'm talking about that time your husband pinched your butt and gave you a wink to remind you of how you would spend the last half hour of your night together.

What if, when I noticed one of these precious moments happening, I gave it a moment? A quick moment of recognition? A prayer of praise for the teeniest thing that just made my life the teeniest, tiniest bit happier?

Rejoice in the Lord always. I will say it again: Rejoice! (Phil. 4:4)

As I said in the last chapter, it's not a matter of being surprised at what God is able to do and has done in my life, but it's a matter of gratitude. Of giving it a moment to simply say thank you for the big stuff *and* the small stuff. Thanksgiving shouldn't be only the National Day of Gluttony at the end of November. It should be an attitude, a matter of intentionally looking and listening for the stuff that makes us feel happy and also the stuff God provides for us when life is anything but.

Like giving an honorary moment of silence. Like taking a minute to soak up all of the big feelings I feel. Like letting my thoughts and feelings and wonderings and praise and prayer and awe linger as long as they want to. Like letting them speak to my heart:

> You make known to me the path of life;
>> you will fill me with joy in your presence,
>> with eternal pleasures at your right hand. (Ps. 16:11)

Much of this broken, hurtful, and painful life on earth is to be mourned, but much of the beauty that finds its way out of the ashes is to be celebrated too. Like a neighbor saying, "Love ya" at the end of your phone conversation. Like realizing you made a new friend.

I love you too, Joan.

To Take This Deeper

Give It a Moment

- **Reflect:** What are some of the little things that you can first thank God for and then celebrate today? Are there any wake-up-and-smell-the-coffee or stop-and-smell-the-roses moments in your life that need their own minute of celebration and thanksgiving?

- **Take Action:** Take a moment to thank God for the big and small stuff He has given you. Take another moment to be a glimmer of happiness to someone else you know, whether it's a phone call to a friend, a note in the mail to a family member, or an invitation to a neighbor. Extend your celebration to those around you.
- **Read:** Read Psalm 136. Celebrate and reiterate this song of thanks to God for both the big and the small things in your life.

Nineteen

Past the Scattered Feminine Hygiene Products

Give Attention

> *Those I came to see were too busy to see me ... but there are times when I just want to be with my people. There are times I want to talk to my people—to hear about their day, to laugh a bit, to cry some. There are times when I just want to be their father.*
>
> —Max Lucado, *The Children of the King*[1]

Pay attention. Have you looked? Have you really looked today?

Yes, Lord, I have looked was my reply. *And do You know what I see? I see a stack of dirty dishes that need to be scrubbed, a bunch of books that need to be reshelved, a ton of toys that need to be put back in their bins. And I see a box of feminine hygiene products that keeps finding its way out of the bathroom cupboard, and its contents are now scattered all over the living room floor. I'm pretty sure You would be able to pick the culprit for that one out of a lineup.*

Pay attention. Have you looked?

Yup, I thought. *Because do You know what else I see, Lord? I see the light on my phone is blinking, meaning I have some sort of e-mail or text or phone call I need to reply to.*

Pay attention.

And watch this grand finale, Lord, I geared up. *Because last but not least, I look in the mirror. And do You know what I see there? I see a greasy-faced, snarly haired, prickly legged, slightly haggard mom who could use a shower and at least a tiny swab of mascara to brighten her tired eyes. And* now *I just stubbed my toe. You know how angry it makes me when I stub my toe! I'm a mess, Lord. Really. When I look around, I see a mess. And when I look at myself, I see a mess. A mess from the outside in.*

Pay attention. Have you looked? Have you really looked today? Do you hear Me saying, "I love you"?

I get it, Lord, I thought, rolling my eyes like an exasperated teenager. *"Jesus loves me, this I know." I have been hearing that my whole life. But what does that have to do with the substantial disaster in our apartment and on my face right now?*

Just look. Pay attention. Really look around and see. See that I love you.

So that's what I did today.

I did my normal mommy stuff, but I also looked. I tried to see past the dirty dishes, the bunch of books, the tons of toys, and the feminine hygiene products strewn all over the living room floor like goose feathers. It was hard. There are so many distractions; I have so much white noise in my life. But today I really looked. I paid attention; I tried to decipher God's "I love yous" by observing my little world. I know He says it, but today I wanted to hear it.

So I watched Baby. I watched God speak to me through our child. And here is what I saw:

I saw her marshmallow legs and cupcake cheeks I wish I could eat for breakfast. I saw her bright blonde hair and deep brown eyes that speak so much of her personality even before she is able to talk. I saw her toothy grin with the goofy teeth that make me wonder if she has been chewing on rocks again lately. And I saw the whole package of how she is the image of her daddy, with just a touch of Mommy's wide ears. And it's all so cute I think I could die.

And when I looked, when I really looked at her, it's like I could feel God whispering, *You, My daughter, are beautiful. You, My child, are a delight. I made you. I created you. While the broken world you live in will remind you that you aren't perfect, I AM. And I don't make mistakes. You are not a mistake. And do you see how you are filled with these great feelings of love and awe and wonder when you look at your daughter? That's just a taste of the big, great, and awesome feelings I have for you. I. Love. You.*

Later, I put my phone on silent and hid it in the other room so I wouldn't even be tempted. I gave Baby a solid twenty minutes of uninterrupted playtime. And while we were playing, Baby brought me one of her books. She crawled into my lap and batted those enormous brown eyes. Her way of saying, "Please read to me, Mommy." And my heart almost couldn't take it.

Because I felt God whisper, *I love spending time with you too. I think it is so great when you come to Me to rest in Me. No bizarre expectations of who you should be or what you should look like. When you come to Me as you are, I am pleased. When you purposefully set aside your distractions to listen to Me, to see and to feel My presence in your life, I am glad.*

And as every amount of quality time with Baby entails, she and I suffered through one of her tantrums for the sole reason of Who Knows Why. I tried to help her, but she wouldn't listen. She couldn't seem to understand that I was on her side, trying to help her. She was at that tough late-baby-early-toddler stage where there is no compromise. There is no bribery, no reasoning. There is no communicating besides, "Something is wrong, Mommy, but I can't tell you what it is!"

But then I felt God whisper, *Does this remind you of anyone you know? Someone who likes to throw tantrums when she doesn't get her way? Someone who struggles with impatience and distrust of a certain other Someone who has it all under control? Learn to trust Me, My child. I am here because I love you and I know what's best for you. Not because I want to see you hurting, frustrated, or angry.*

And as the day went on, I saw more and more. Baby fell down and cried. I drew her into my embrace and held her securely in my arms. God saying, *I know it hurts. It hurts Me too. But I'm here to hold you, to comfort you. Let Me cry with you, and then let Me wipe away your tears. Let Me show you that you are going to be okay and that I will carry you through this.*

Baby tried her hand at coloring. She took a blank piece of paper and made marks with bright colored pencils all across the page. The Father delighting, *I love seeing you use your gifts. I love seeing you be creative. I love seeing you find enjoyment in the world around you. In the world I created.*

And later, when my phone found its way back into my

hands, blinking and beeping and begging for me to quickly get something done, Baby screamed and swatted it down again.

Be present. This matters. This, right here in front of you, matters.

God speaks. In the ordinary, in the everyday. And not just through what I think of as the spiritual things in life. He speaks in the tangible, in the physical. He is not just the God of pencil and paper and bookbindings and church buildings. He is the God of nature. He is the God of my human flesh. He is the God of an entire creation that tells me how majestic and mighty He really is. "The heavens declare the glory of God; the skies proclaim the work of his hands. Day after day they pour forth speech; night after night they reveal knowledge" (Ps. 19:1–2).

He is the God of my senses. He speaks through the things I see, hear, taste, touch, and smell. I taste His grace when I take, eat, and drink the bread and wine of Communion, as I remember and believe Christ's holy sacrifice and salvation. "Taste and see that the LORD is good; blessed is the one who takes refuge in him" (Ps. 34:8).

I smell His goodness when my friend shares her gift of hospitality topped with a heaping plate of something Italian. "Follow God's example, therefore, as dearly loved children and walk in the way of love, just as Christ loved us and gave himself up for us as a fragrant offering and sacrifice to God" (Eph. 5:1–2).

I hear His mercy when I sit in the church pew, listening to the pastor remind me week after week that I am welcome there, even though I am imperfect and in need of a Savior. "Listen, you heavens, and I will speak; hear, you earth, the words of my mouth. Let my teaching fall like rain and my words descend like dew, like showers on new grass, like abundant rain on tender plants" (Deut. 32:1–2).

I feel His unconditional love when Husband gives me that look and pulls me into his strong arms. That look reminds me he chose to stick by me for better or for ugly, even when I'm the haggard mess I am today, from the outside in. "Husbands, love your wives, just as Christ loved the church and gave himself up for her" (Eph. 5:25).

And I see God's generous provision everywhere. When I look—that is, when I *really* look. I might only see a pile of dirty dishes, a bunch of books, a ton of toys, and a box of feminine hygiene products strewn all over the house, but what if that's God whispering His love and kindness?

Look at the abundance I have provided for you. That pile of laundry? I told you that you are worth more to Me than the sparrows. Those dishes you need to scrape the leftover crumbs off of? I told you I would provide your daily bread. The cleaning and scrubbing you dislike so passionately? A reminder of the good health you have been given and are working to maintain. The e-mails and phone calls and texts you need to reply to? Friends, family, community, and opportunity.

Maybe I need to stop looking at life through a lens and look with my eyes, if only for a moment. Maybe I need to give my child the gift of my undivided presence among all the chores, if only for a half hour. Because maybe if I'm paying attention, even on normal-mom days, I'll have the opportunity to learn more about God's unconditional love for me, His child. It's a matter of looking and listening for His voice, of tasting and smelling and feeling His presence in my life.

Oh, Kendra? I forgot one other thing. That toe you stubbed earlier? You stubbed that on the wall of the apartment you live in. You lucky girl.

To Take This Deeper

Give Attention

- **Reflect:** Have you looked? Have you *really* looked today? Do you hear God saying, "I love you"? When you pay attention to what you see, hear, taste, smell, and touch, what is God saying? How is He taking care of you in ways you don't always recognize or appreciate?

- **Take Action:** Think through the mundane and monotonous parts of your day. Remind yourself of how God says, "I love you" in those moments. Thank Him, and pay that message forward to your spouse, your child, your neighbor, or your friend.

- **Read:** Read John 10:1–21. Listen to the Good Shepherd's voice as He speaks to you and beckons you to follow Him. Because the Good Shepherd *loves you*.

Golf and Power Outages

Give It Up, Ya Loser

Online life is no substitute for
practiced, physical presence.

—Jen Hatmaker, *For the Love*[1]

Husband is a golf enthusiast. When he was a toddler, his dad sawed off old clubs and wrapped the ends with electrical tape for him to use. Eventually he played golf in college. And now we spend one weekend every spring watching The Masters golf tournament on TV. As in, one of us watches and the other one naps. It's true love.

But do you want to know what is true sacrifice, something that could possibly be placed in the category called Sustained Torture? Actually going out and golfing eighteen holes. It's agony, doing the same thing over and over with the same slice and the same divots and the same twenty-seven shots it takes me to get the ball to the pin on a par-five hole. Every time I swing, I hear that sad little turtle from the animated movie

Cats Don't Dance: "There's no use trying. Last night my fortune cookie said, 'Give it up, ya *loser*.'"[2]

I can do a round of nine holes of golf with a smile, with enthusiasm, and with pure enjoyment, but may the good Lord spare me from the persecution that is eighteen holes of golf. Because that is exactly what we were doing on that October Saturday, in the cold, in the rain.

Want to know what added insult to injury? This was a date. We did something we rarely do and hired a babysitter for a few hours, and our date was eighteen holes of golf. How incredibly romantic. In Husband's defense, we were playing in a tournament to benefit the Sports Boosters at his school. But *eighteen holes.*

All the way from our apartment to the golf course that morning I prayed, *Father, if You are willing, take these eighteen cups from me.*

And now that I am done complaining, let me explain what I actually loved about this date: the little invention of golf carts. I would've had to be dragged kicking and cursing from our vehicle if we'd had to golf eighteen holes in the cold rain *and* walk the entire way, but being in a golf cart together for four hours was a completely different story. Suddenly we were taking little cruises here and there and having chopped-up conversations between everyone else's swings, chips, and putts. We were enjoying a four-hour session of spousal bonding, making real connections with the number one really important person in our lives. We were doing something together that didn't involve sitting in front of a screen like a couple zombies who seemed to have forgotten why they even like each other. So, of course, I couldn't get enough of *that.*

Let me clearly state that we are nowhere near being

anti-TV. We mooch off my parents' Netflix account more than I'd like to admit, and if we won the lottery, we would delegate a slice for weekly movie tickets, buttered popcorn, and babysitters. I'm just realizing more and more the importance of making real connections with real people *without* a screen in front of our faces or on our laps or in our hands. We need to learn to be present with the people sitting right in front of us instead of obsessing over what's happening outside the room we're in. Instead of binge watching through life.

I think about the correlation between All My Time and Screen Time a lot, partially because I give much of my time to social media for both work and entertainment. Partially because, as Jen Hatmaker wrote in her book *For the Love*, "we live in a strange, unprecedented time when face-to-face relationships are becoming optional."[3] While social media might take up a chunk of All My Time, it simply can't replace making real connections with real people. Hatmaker continued,

> People crave what they have always craved: to be known
> and loved, to belong somewhere. . . . If Jesus' basic march-
> ing orders were 1) to love God and 2) to love people, then
> the fruit of that obedience includes being loved by God
> and loved by people. We give and get here. According to
> Jesus, the love of God and people is the substance of life.[4]

As strange as it is to admit now, one thing I miss most about living in Guatemala is the frequent power outages, how we would be left in the dark and off the grid for hours at a time: No computers. No Wi-Fi. No TV. No lesson planning. No books unless we used our hiking headlamps or the flashlights on our not-smartphones. All Husband and I could really do at eight o'clock on a pitch-black Tuesday night was sit and talk and . . . um, you know, that one *other* thing. We have never had such great pillow talk. It was seriously so incredibly romantic.

We dreamed about the future. We gave back rubs. We talked about the embarrassing and tricky stuff in our marriage that's hard to talk about in broad daylight. We solved all of Guatemala's political, socioeconomical, and spiritual problems and went on to fix the United States' as well. We talked about our personal struggles and victories. We stopped talking and enjoyed each other's presence in the quiet darkness. We fell asleep at a decent hour. Incredibly romantic, yes, but also incredibly rejuvenating for all people, not just introverts.

We think we have come so far as a society, which we have: our technology, our science, our apps, all of it—just, wow. But for how advanced we have become, it sure feels like we have backtracked in other ways: our eye contact, our presence, our community. It's amazing the stuff you can do through a screen or on the Internet, but there's still so much you *can't* do with either of those things. You can't bear-hug or French kiss. You can't eat double-chocolate-fudge-brownie ice cream or take a fifteen-minute power nap. You can't snuggle your baby, or take a bubble bath, or feel the warm sun on your bare shoulders, or get the perfect haircut. You can't say "cheers" and clink a glass of wine with your friend. You can't play eighteen holes of golf with your hubby.

Being stripped of all distractions during those power outages in Guatemala helped us realize something important: sometimes we need to give things up in order to let other things in our lives grow, to let other things in our lives thrive.

Sometimes the message comes not from a sad little turtle on an animated movie but God nudging our hearts: *Give it up.* I'm not only talking screens and Internet either. Lots of things hinder us from making real connections with real people.

Stuff. Our heinous amount of stuff, our constant search for more stuff, and the amount of time it takes to maintain our stuff. Where did we get the idea that we should fill our homes with stuff that doesn't serve a purpose, is never used, and doesn't bring joy to us or others? "Stuff" is partially a personal-preference thing. I personally prefer to be on the OCD, minimalist, zero-clutter side of the spectrum. And I have many friends and family who feel, live, and thrive otherwise. It's not that our stuff is bad, but, as some of the richest people in the world, we can bring more intention to our purchases, to what we choose to give money, space, time, and maintenance to in our homes and lives, simply because we can. On her blog *Nourishing Minimalism*, Rachel Jones wrote of her journey to declutter her family's life:

> And I looked around at everything we have and it struck me, how we have so much *stuff* that we spend all our time *taking care of it and getting more of it* and we think *nothing* of other people in our neighborhood, city, state, country or world. . . . What if I got rid of everything that distracts me and changed my neighborhood into a community where everyone knows everyone . . . ?[5]

Schedules. Our overcommitted calendars that stretch us in too many unhealthy directions. I said this before: I like committing to doing a few things well. I don't like committing to a million things half-hiney. It's not good for me, and it's not good for the millions of people I'm half-hiney committed to either. Before I commit 110 percent of myself to everyone and their garden gnomes, I need to remember that giving 110 percent of anything is mathematically impossible. I can't do it all.

And sometimes I try to make life *too* organized, *too* busy, *too* scheduled to let life flow and create space for people. For sitting on the porch with a glass of wine on a warm summer's eve, and then on the next open night to think, *Hey, let's invite our neighbors over for a glass of wine out on the porch on this warm summer's eve.* Sometimes it takes scheduling to make community happen; sometimes it takes putting the all-consuming schedule aside.

Sin. All sin is bad. But some sins can absolutely demolish relationships if never brought to the light and addressed with grace: porn, drug or alcohol abuse, emotional or physical abuse, extramarital affairs.

Attitude. Maybe what I need to let go of is unnecessary guilt for saying no to that one commitment that would have pushed my sanity over the cliff. Maybe it's a dangerous attitude of pride for keeping up with the Joneses and all their stuff. Maybe it's a self-conscious attitude of fear, or a sour attitude of "I don't feel like it" about doing something I don't particularly enjoy, even though it is a great way to bond with someone I care about. (*Cough, cough, golfing eighteen holes.*)

Give it up, ya loser.

Lord, now is really not the time to be criticizing my putting stance, I grumbled. *But I get it. Just like You're telling me to, I'll give it up and realize the gift in this day: the golf course before me, the golf cart behind me, and the husband beside me. And that last one—he's totally worth giving up a little warmth to spend quality time with today.*

Therefore, since we are surrounded by such a great cloud of witnesses, let us throw off everything that hinders and the sin that so easily entangles. And let us run with perseverance the race marked out for us. (Heb. 12:1)

So I think about what I can give up that hinders real connections with the real people in my life. I think about putting the phone down, about shutting the TV off, about getting rid of "it," about just saying no, about shedding that attitude.

I think about how I was out there on a golf course with frozen hands and a runny nose, playing eighteen holes in the cold October rain, driving and slicing and shanking and trying to keep from cursing, but also loving the precious quality time with the man I truly like.

In a world that values stuff, impossible schedules, and superficial relationships, we have to fight extra hard to give time to the real people in our lives. If we want our relationships to last as long as we are breathing, that means carving out space to breathe. So many other things will fade in this life, and what's left are the people you took time to shoot a few holes of golf with.

To Take This Deeper

Give It Up, Ya Loser

- **Reflect:** Who are some of the people who make up the core tribe of your life? Is there anything you should give up in order to foster real connections with them? Remember that sometimes we need to give up things in order to let other things in our lives thrive.

- **Take Action:** Carve out some quality time with someone from your core tribe. Use that time to do something at least one of you enjoys doing, to foster real connection with each other that doesn't involve a screen.
- **Read:** Read Psalm 39:4–7. Use the short time we have on earth in purposeful ways: purposefully connecting with the real people in our lives, purposefully throwing off things that hinder, purposefully putting our hope in the Lord.

Twenty-One

Would the Neighborhood Miss Us?

Give Someone a Hand

> *Sunday morning in church is the one place*
> *where evangelism cannot take place in our*
> *generation, because the lost are not there.*
>
> —Tim Chester and Steve Timmis, *Everyday Church*[1]

We were sitting in another church pew, and I was fighting back tears.

When I woke up and ate my peanut butter toast for breakfast, when I showered and put on my bright coral dress, warm leggings, and brown boots, I didn't prepare for Church Crying. But it was one of those sermons that struck a chord in my heart, a chord that felt like harmony, not the random pounding of Baby's hands on her little play keyboard.

We were still searching for a congregation to call home, and it was still slightly exhausting. Part of the reason was because I was tired of being a hater, of being critical, of being angry at everything.

I knew it was just a required step for reentry after living outside the United States of America for an extended amount of time. In fact, I'm pretty sure customs just stamped *Haters* on the first empty space in our passports. We were in the process of reestablishing ourselves in our birth culture from the one we had just spent three years learning and loving. We were measuring everything we grew up knowing to everything we had just seen. And we were wondering how to handle the stuff that didn't seem to add up anymore. Especially when it came to the church. Some of our deepest criticisms were toward the first-world church.

After moving back, we had visited one church that had two big screens up during their service with crazy screen-saver designs flashing all over them, while the words of the songs were displayed on two entirely different screens. It felt like a middle school skating party, like the song "I'm a Barbie Girl in a Barbie World" should be playing in the background instead of "Amazing Grace." Enter criticism: *Are those two extra screens really necessary? Who approved those to be in the church's budget?*

One church we visited did not say a single "welcome," "hello," or "Christ is risen; He is risen indeed." Enter criticism: *Do they realize how cold it felt to enter and leave their building? What if we weren't Christians? What if we hadn't been to church for a really long time?*

One church we visited had a variety of programs for those already part of the congregation, but when we asked about outreach, we received lots of, "Um . . . well . . . you see . . ." Enter criticism: *I can't even.*

We had a vision of the type of congregation we wanted to join. We wanted simplicity over entertainment. We wanted worship over fluff. We wanted prayer over planning. We wanted giving over keeping. We wanted looking outside the doors just as much as focusing inward. We wanted biblical truth over personal relativism. But right then, when our focus was on the imperfections of congregations rather than the unity of Christ's body, we were part of the problem. When our criticisms and hostility and hatred toward congregations surpassed our desire to love and grow with and be a part of the church, then we were just a couple of know-it-alls. A couple of blow bags, to put it nicely.

And that's why I was choking back tears and trying to swallow a big lump in my throat. The preacher was giving a sermon about their church learning to have a bigger impact on its very own neighborhood. His words reminded me that we were not the only ones who felt a fire and wanted to show God's love to the people we crossed paths with every day. There was no need for us to have an Elijah complex where we thought we were the only ones left who wished to be faithful to the Lord (1 Kings 19:10).

His sermon was softening my heart, interrupting my hateful criticism: *They want to be faithful disciples too. You are not alone. You're all in this together.*

The sermon began with a pretend news article that imagined the church had exploded from a gas leak and burned to the ground. Neighbors who lived next to the church were interviewed after the accident:

"They seemed like nice people. . . . Never really talked to any of them; sort of kept to themselves . . ."

"I always wondered what it looked like inside, you know, but none of us in the neighborhood got invited to the Open House. At least I wasn't . . ."

"They'd have the windows open from time to time. Really liked when they sang 'They'll Know We Are Christians by Our Love.'"[2]

The article and quotes were pretend, but the preacher's follow-up questions were not:

Is [our church] good news for this neighborhood? I'm sure we're not bad news. We're neat and tidy neighbors. We care about our property and don't usually spit on the sidewalk. But what if we're not good news, or bad news, just no news? If [our church] were to disappear, would anyone in [our city] notice? . . . Would anyone miss us after over fifty years of living in this community? Are we something like the common reaction of neighbors to the discovery that a serial killer lived right next door for years: "He seemed like a nice guy. Always said, 'Hello.' Kept to himself. Never really bothered me."[3]

I was moved that there were others out there who recognized the important job of *going out* and *reaching out* in our own neighborhoods. Of taking the steps to get to know our neighbors and sharing Christ's love with them in a way that showed God's big grace is so very bountiful. Of being the kind of churches where our neighborhoods could say more than, "They seemed like nice people."

Going out. Reaching out. Getting to know. *Giving a hand.* Recognizing, like Tim Chester and Steve Timmis wrote in their book *Everyday Church*, that our modes of outreach desperately need to be revised:

> We can no longer think of church as a meeting on a Sunday morning. We must think of church as a community of people who share life, ordinary life. And we cannot think of mission as an event that takes place in an ecclesiastical building. Of course, there will continue to be a role for special events, but the bedrock of mission will be ordinary life. . . . An everyday church with an everyday mission.[4]

"An everyday church with an everyday mission"—being so focused on the gospel in our everyday lives that, as in the church of Thessalonica, our faith, hope, and love would naturally pour out and into the lives of our neighbors, coworkers, and acquaintances at our kids' baseball practices.

The pastor's sermon continued:

> This is faith as vocation, as lifestyle, work that proceeds from grace. This labor of love and work of faith has less to do with feeling and more to do with intention, action, the things we choose to do as a demonstration that the gift of grace leads somewhere. The church at Thessalonica was an example of this, a type, a pattern. Somehow the church collectively as a community was a type for others to follow and imitate.[5]

Outreach is not to be confused with an extensive list of church programs and activities. Outreach is everyday life. Before we left for Guatemala, we were told over and over, "There is a mission field right here in the United States, too, you know," and I believe that with all my mind. So now that we were back in the United States, I didn't want to neglect the mission field that was right here. I wanted to share the bounty of grace God had given me with the people in my everyday circles of life: my child, my friends, my neighbors, strangers in passing. And I wanted us to find a congregation to join that recognized the opportunity to bring Christ's bright light to those around them too.

> We tend to measure a church's impact on quantifiable things these days: the number of members, the health of the budget, square footage, number of programs or staff. Yet Paul had no such formula. He cited the reputation of the church at Thessalonica for their work of faith and labor of love.[6]

So I asked myself too: Would the neighborhood miss us? Not *us* actually, but Christ's presence *within us*?

We had been there for only a few months, and relationships take time. But if we lived there awhile longer and either death parted us or a move relocated us, would the neighborhood miss us? Would people notice that Christ's light within us had left our apartment building? Would Joan say, "Good riddance"? Would Jim say, "I asked them for help one time, and they never got back to me"? Would Josh and Christina say, "They seemed like nice people, but they never invited us over for dinner or to hang out or anything"?

People won't always respond to Jesus People with delight and acceptance. Neighbors won't always be thrilled with our efforts to get to know them. Acquaintances won't always accept our invitations. Scripture shows Jesus was compassionate and

He spoke the truth. He not only seemed like a nice person; He *was* a nice person. But He was still despised, rejected, mocked, beaten, and crucified. Should I expect any less as one of His followers?

Loving our neighbors is truly a reckless lifestyle. Scripture tells us to love but to expect hatred in return; to give but to expect no repayment. We are asked to be servants in a land of entitlement. In a place where we are told to do our best to live comfortably, here is the good Lord stretching us outside of the comfortable boxes we'd like to leave ourselves in. No matter our personality traits—whether being around people energizes or drains us—giving all our love and expecting absolutely nothing in return is not the norm. But this reckless love that springs so abundantly from Christ is what overpowers the anxiety of facing what might appear to be a bogus cause.

But my job is not to make other people believe in the work I am doing or in the Savior I represent. That work is beyond me. My job is to show, to share, to love, to pray, to give someone a hand. To be a light in this desperately dark world, within the everyday circumstances I find myself in.

As the sermon concluded, it's all about grace:

> And here's the deal: grace receivers soon become grace givers, grace spreaders. Faith is always personal, but never private. Grace builds a faith community that lives in relation to those around it. It is possible to reach into the community around us, the people that surround us. A life lived fully is contagiously hopeful.[7]

The goal of the church of Thessalonica wasn't to keep up their reputation or to receive people's praise or for their physical presence to be missed. Their goal was that their "work produced by faith, [their] labor prompted by love, and [their] endurance inspired by hope in our Lord Jesus Christ" (1 Thess. 1:3) would bring praise to God's name and spread word of *His* reputation to the ends of the earth.

And their example is an exciting invitation for all disciples of Christ—not just for one small congregation but for the entire body. It's an invitation full of love, joy, and hope; full of enthusiasm, endurance, and perseverance. An invitation rooted so deeply in the gospel that we can't help but let the gospel pour out from our own lives into others'—by being present in our own neighborhoods, by giving people a hand in our communities, by sharing Christ's love in the opportunities we are given.

It's an invitation that brought me to tears and prodded me to look around in camaraderie, rather than in angry criticism, toward the people we were sharing the pews with. Criticism—even cleansing fire—has its place, but so do encouragement, support, and brotherly love.

They want to be faithful disciples too. You are not alone. You're all in this together.

The work of outreach might be tiring and slow. The people we try to love might even hate us in return. But we are the church, and when we let the gospel take deep root in us and transform our own lives, we can then *be* that blessed church toward others. We can do this together: serve together, look outside of our doors together, lend a helping hand in our neighborhoods together.

Not just *seem* like nice people, but *be* the light of Christ's presence. The light of Christ's presence that people would miss if it left.

To Take This Deeper
Give Someone a Hand

- **Reflect:** How can you, within the context of your everyday life, be purposeful in outreach? Who are the people you come into contact with who could benefit from Christ's light within you?
- **Take Action:** Take action to be a kind and compassionate person toward someone in your everyday life. Whether someone asks you for help, or you know someone who could use your help, take steps to show the gospel through your kindness.
- **Read:** Read Matthew 5:13–16. "Let your light shine" (v. 16) so that others will respond in praise to God.

Chicken Soup for My Soul

Give Freely

The world's way of pursuing riches is grasping
and hoarding. You attain My riches by
letting go and giving. The more you give
yourself to Me and My ways, the more I fill
you with inexpressible, heavenly Joy.

—Sarah Young, *Jesus Calling*[1]

I love driving up the highway and seeing that big, blue *Welcome to Pure Michigan* sign.

One of the many perks of being a stay-at-home mom is you can say, "Let's pack up and go to Grandpa and Grandma's house for a couple days and get a change of scenery." So that's where Baby and I were headed to spend the next week. She likes to go for the dogs and cats. I like to go for the food and cocktails and laughter that happen around my parents' kitchen table.

My dad prophesied that once I left Michigan for college, I would never return, and so far he's a pretty legit prophet. But

I love Michigan, not because of the Great Lakes or sand dunes or trees or blueberries or Hudsonville ice cream or summer sunshine. I love it because it's where I was raised, where I was shaped. Because it's family. No matter where Husband and I live, travel to, or create a home for our own family, a tiny piece of my heart will always think of Michigan as home. I probably sound like a sappy country song, but really, it's like chicken soup for my soul every time I get to go back.

It takes roughly two hours and twenty minutes to drive from our apartment in South Chicago to my parents' house in Grand Rapids. And that day's drive, the anticipation, the memories—all like a steaming hot bowl of chicken noodle soup on a crisp autumn day—warmed my insides and reminded me how insanely rich my life has been.

So often I think of Wealth and its ugly cousin, Poverty, in simple terms of money. But they are so, so much more complicated than that. They are more like intricately woven webs, dependent on and affected by many things: resources, relationships, identity.[2] Some aspects of Wealth and Poverty are the result of our own choices, some are the result of choices others made before us, and some have absolutely nothing to do with choice.

I am rich. I could talk in simple terms of money: We live off one Christian-schoolteacher salary, yet we are in the wealthiest 8.8 percent of the world's population.[3] We are able to afford basic needs like food, clothes, and monthly rent, and every once in a while things like going out to eat, seeing a movie at the theater, and buying gas to go to Michigan and all the other places our families live. Some months we are even able to save a couple dollars for whatever we might need in the future. *Wow, I am rich.*

But Wealth is more than money.

As we were in the car, crossing over the Indiana border, I thought about my parents, who have loved each other for more than thirty-one years, who tenderly raised me for eighteen years. And I felt God asking me, nudging me to see: *Do you recognize the wealth of having parents who make it easy for you to understand the metaphor "God the Father"? Who give you a taste of My own great love for you?*

As we took in the *Welcome to Pure Michigan* sign, I thought about my four sisters and one brother, whom I have bickered with, quoted a million movies with, road-tripped with, and ganged up on our parents with my entire life. And I felt God asking me to realize: *Do you recognize the wealth of being able to genuinely label your family as friends? How even though you all do life differently, you still find common ground and deep love and laughter around your parents' table?*

As we got on Interstate 196 toward Grand Rapids, I thought about how I was able to complete eighteen years of education. I can read and write and even had the chance to earn a bachelor's degree in elementary education. When I thought about what I wanted to be when I grew up, I had the luxury of choosing a job that would pay the bills *and* a job that I would enjoy doing. And I heard God whispering for me to understand: *Do you recognize the wealth of these types of opportunities, of these choices you had the privilege of making?*

As we pulled into my parents' driveway, I realized I could go on and on like this:

I have a husband who not only has chosen to love me for all the days of his life but also seems to sincerely like me. I have a healthy, beautiful daughter who is full of perk and spunk. I have friends who have been positive influences since kindergarten. Besides chicken pox, a few cases of the flu, and morning sickness, I have had a clean bill of health. And don't even get me started on how my in-laws *don't* make my life a nightmare. *Wow, I am rich.*

This all used to make me feel guilty: the place, the family, the wealth I was born into. When I returned to the United States from spending three weeks in Uganda, the only thing I could do as I transitioned from what people casually call "culture shock" was lay on my bed and cry. The poverty *was* shocking; the devastation *was* overwhelming. But the entire experience was awakening.

Poverty and devastation were the reality I had to recognize outside the bubble of my safe and mostly happy life. Seeing the third world in Uganda and eventually living in the third world in Guatemala helped me start wrestling through my initial questions like, "Why them, and why not me?" and eventually move on to more important questions like, "What can I do to get involved?" I finally recognized my extreme wealth after staring extreme poverty in the face. And recognition is usually the first step to recovery. There's a great disconnect: between the first and the third worlds, yes, but between the Uppers and the Lowers of *all* worlds.

I described my past, my family, and my upbringing like chicken soup for my soul. I could just as easily use words like *happy, loved,* and *full.* But part of me wants to stop right there and hug whoever is reading this thinking, *No, that is* not *my life. That was not my upbringing. Chicken soup for my soul? My family—whom I don't like, who hurt me—are more like cat-meat tacos for my gut.* Happy, loved, full? *Try* lonely, rejected, hungry.

I could try to imagine all of it being taken from me—my privileged upbringing, my supportive family, my abundance of possessions and opportunities. I could try to imagine all I had left was the sweatshirt on my back, a cardboard box on the street, and the scraps of bread from someone's restaurant leftovers. But I admit that, hard as I try, attempting to put myself in someone else's underprivileged, tattered, hungry shoes is still only imagination.

It's not that my life has been all roses. I'm not trying to paint the picture that my family and I have lived a Ken-and-Barbie life, free from all hardships. We have experienced grief; we have felt tough consequences related to our bad choices. We have had strained relationships. We have suffered heart-breaks, wrestled with fear and jealousy. Among ourselves we have had seasons of arguments and rivalry and bitterness. My dad used to say, "We put the 'fun' in 'dysfunctional.'" But as I venture out and meet more people, I continue to realize that even being able to look back and say "mostly good" about my past is a rarity.

One of my biggest struggles has been my self-image. Growing up, I had low self-esteem tied to feeling awkward in my own body. I was the sweaty six-year-old who had to learn to put on deodorant before she put on her Barney backpack. I was the unfortunate eight-year-old with an overbite who had to sport headgear to school. I was the goofy-looking thirteen-year-old with braces and greasy-faced acne. I was the lanky sixteen-year-old who played volleyball and got nicknamed Giraffe by two different opposing teams.

Thank the Lord I can laugh about it all now. But as I grew up, my self-esteem shifted from being based on my body image to being based on my accomplishments, rooting itself in my successes and failures as an athlete, a teacher, a wife, a mom, a writer.

My struggle with self-esteem isn't the result of lackluster parental support. I can't even count the times I heard my parents say, "I love you," "You are beautiful," and "We are your biggest fans." But my struggle with self-esteem points to a different kind of poverty: a poverty of *identity* I experience when I try to find my worth in anything other than Christ. Because finding my worth in anything other than Christ will always fail; always disappoint; always leave me feeling low, unworthy, unwanted, ugly, impoverished.

But grace is where rich and poor unite. It's where those classified as "wealthy" realize that eventually moth and rust will destroy all forms of their earthly possessions. It's where those without even a cup of water are offered living water that will satisfy their needs for all eternity. It's where our identities are restored.

I love how Paul—the man with the privileged upbringing, who gave it all up for a life of persecution and imprisonment as God's missionary to the Gentiles—correlated God's grace with riches.

> In him we have redemption through his blood, the forgiveness of sins, in accordance with the *riches of God's grace* that he lavished on us. . . . And God raised us up with Christ and seated us with him in the heavenly realms in Christ Jesus, in order that in the coming ages he might show the *incomparable riches of his grace*, expressed in his kindness to us in Christ Jesus. (Eph. 1:7–8, 2:6–7, emphasis added)

And I love how Peter described the welcomed, wanted, beautiful, rich identity that *all* have through salvation. An identity rooted only in Christ's deep love for us.

But you are a *chosen* people, a *royal* priesthood, a *holy* nation, God's *special* possession, that you may declare the praises of him who called you out of darkness into his wonderful light. (1 Peter 2:9, emphasis added)

The best gift God ever gave us is grace. My privileged upbringing, my supportive family, my abundance of possessions and opportunities—none of those things can save me from eternal hell and separation from God. But God, in His rich mercy and grace, has offered us salvation, regardless of our upbringings or the amount of possessions and opportunities we have.

In Matthew 10, Jesus sent out His twelve disciples to the people of Israel. He stated that their mission was to preach that the kingdom of heaven was near, drive out evil spirits, and heal diseases. Then He said, "Freely you have received; freely give" (Matt. 10:8). The disciples freely received power to preach and heal. I have freely received an abundance of resources and emotional support.

As I walked through my parents' front door, hauling Baby and our bags of stuff for the week, I recognized that life's riches are God's love, poured out for me. But God also calls me to action as a person of wealth in an impoverished world: *Did you see all this, Daughter? You have freely received. Not only an abundance of possessions from My hands but also the riches of grace from My Son's sacrifice. What will your reaction be? How will you choose to freely give just like I first freely gave to you?*

There is danger in it, too, this abundance of wealth.

It's easy to just say thank you, make long lists of what I am thankful for during the month of November, and put a #Blessed next to my pictures on Instagram. It's easy to get entrapped by the love of money and stuff. It's easy to focus too much on the "Why them, and why not me?" question and forget to shift to the more important question of "How can I be a part of God's recovering, redemptive story while we await Christ's return?" It's easy to see someone's poverty as a reason for my own gratitude rather than an opportunity to share. It's easy to be so attached to the good things of this world that I forget to remember Uganda, or that man panhandling on the street, or that neighbor who could really use a friend. It's easy to freely receive without freely giving in return.

I see God's actions of giving, giving, giving in my life. All the warm, fuzzy chicken-soup-for-the-soul stuff that to me is summed up in the word *Michigan*. All the ways He uses the tough, grueling, heartbreaking stuff to mold me into the person He desires me to be. And I hear Him asking what my response will be: *Will you show appreciation? Gratitude? Will you be a good steward of these gifts? Will you share, even sacrifice? Will you work to bridge the gap of disconnect between the Uppers and Lowers of the world around you? Will you humbly bow before Me and say, "Yes, Lord, I have freely received. Now I will choose to freely give"?*

As I once again gathered in my parents' kitchen with family, boisterous sounds of life filled the room. It felt good to hug my big, teddy-bear brother and quote lines from *Home Alone*. It felt right to sit around the table with my sisters, a glass of peach Moscato in each of our hands and laughter filling each of our hearts. My throat caught a little, grateful for the wealth of love from people who make pure Michigan feel like home. Grateful for the reminder of all I have freely and undeservingly received in this world.

Wow, I am rich.

To Take This Deeper

Give Freely

- **Reflect:** In what ways do you see yourself as wealthy or poor in resources, relationships, and identity? In what ways can you freely give just as you have freely received?

- **Take Action:** After reflecting on wealth and poverty in your own life with the questions above, consider how you can take a leap of faith to give of what you have in abundance, even to the point of sacrifice.

- **Read:** Read Matthew 25:14–30. Put the gifts that God has given you to good use. Remember while reading the parable of the talents that it was never about *how much* each servant was first given, but always about *how faithful* each was with what he was given.

Give the Gift of Stress This Christmas

Give Gifts

*We are once again spending money
we don't have on things we don't
need to give to people we don't like.*

—Stephen Colbert[1]

Every year my family and I have the same conversation roughly one to two months before Christmas: How are we going to handle buying presents for each other during the holidays?

I have strong opinions about Christmas presents. We have a way of ruining a perfectly good holiday with the stress we put on our calendars or finances or emotions in the quest to buy the perfect gifts for people who already have everything. It doesn't help that I am a horrible gift giver—just ask every person I have ever been Secret Santa to. ("Would a candy bar from the gas station wrapped in a sticky note be high on your wish list?") It also doesn't help that my love language is not gifts. ("How about your gift to *me* is that I don't have to buy a gift for *you*, mm-kay, pumpkin?")

But Jiminy Christmas. I feel like the tradition of giving gifts for the holidays has gone a little haywire. I mean, let's talk Black Friday for two secs. On *The Colbert Report*, Stephen Colbert called Black Friday the "holiest" day of the year, when "Americans come together to bow before their lord, the Walmart rollback guy. 'Cause Jesus isn't the only one who saves."[2]

I laugh because it's satire, but I cry a little because it's true. How is it that one day after we say, "Gracious Lord, thank You for the abundance You have blessed us with," we say, "I need more! More! More! At three in the morning! And I will throat-punch your grandma to be the first in line to get more!"

Ironic? Sick? Wrong?

I once wrote a blog post called "Christmas: It's Not Our Birthday Party,"[3] the point being Christmas gifts have a way of making me think this holiday is all about me and mine. They have a way of instilling the attitude of "I deserve this" and leading me to think I should expect to receive gifts. But "deserve" and "expect" strip away the actual meaning of the word *gift* and make it sound a lot more like the word *payment*.

Christmas gifts also have a way of manipulating my mind to turn wants into needs. When I make my Christmas list, I try to think of stuff I need, and when I can't think of anything, I try to think of stuff I want, and then the stuff I want picks at my brain until I am convinced that I need it. But I know that when I truly need something, I go out and buy it without waiting until Christmas. I know it takes a lot of convincing to look at my piles of Christmas gifts and honestly say, "I needed that."

I just hate how we have made celebrating the holidays so darn complicated. Since when wasn't it enough to enjoy one another's presence and conversation and laughter? Since when wasn't it enough to soak up what was already the Gift to us—*the birth of our Savior*?

Now, the Great Christmas-Gift Debate is something to argue about only with the people who claim Luke 2 in their lives, whose purpose for celebrating *Christmas* is to rejoice in the birth of Jesus. This is not something to argue about with the people whose purpose for celebrating *the holidays* is to take a picture with Santa and eat honey-baked ham. Those are two very different groups who are not thinking from the same starting point of Scripture.

But as Christians, as people who know that Christ's birth involved a stable, a few people, a couple of animals, a manger filled with hay, good news of great joy, a host of angels, and almost nothing else, I feel like we should be a little more leery of how much time, emotion, and money we put into the upkeep of our Christmas traditions. Maybe the extent of our traditional Christmas money spending and stuff accumulating should make us feel a little more uncomfortable. In his book *Under the Overpass*, Mike Yankoski wrote,

> Be relentlessly suspicious of your comfortable life, and of the comfort zones that render so many Christian fellowships insensitive and ineffective in our communities. God calls us all to more. And you and I can lead the way, one small step at a time.[4]

In some ways, haven't our Christmas traditions become a comfort zone where we think it's okay to spend and hoard for ourselves? God says things like, "Do not store up for yourselves treasures on earth" (Matt. 6:19), and "Sell your possessions and give to the poor" (Luke 12:33), and "If we have food and clothing, we will be content with that" (1 Tim. 6:8). So why do I think that Christmas gives me the right to throw all that out the window? What if we could do *differently* as families and as the church?

Now, I realize Black Friday does not fully represent Christmas-gift giving or giving gifts in general. I realize that some people's love language *is* gifts, and that there is nothing wrong with feeling loved when someone buys you the perfect gift. I realize that some people have an amazing talent at finding the perfect gifts, at the perfect time, with the perfect attitude. I realize that it is good to give good things to our children. I realize that giving gifts, like any kind of giving, requires sacrifices of our time, emotions, and finances. I realize I have zero control over grandparents who like to spoil their grandchildren. And finally, I realize, as my dear friend said so perfectly, "Giving for the holidays is not just for the spiritually immature who don't care about the third world."

But I'm in search of simplicity here, and I'm in search of answers to a few questions: Are we sacrificing things we shouldn't be—like our sanity—in the name of Christmas tradition? Are we focusing too much on satisfying our own family's *wants* instead of fulfilling another family's *needs*? Contrary to Colbert's quote before the chapter, I do like my family and my family likes one another. Which helped us have that candid conversation about how we wanted to handle Christmas-gift giving that year. Which helped us talk about where our gift giving was appropriate and where we could redirect our giving instead.

Gift giving can't always be avoided, but it doesn't have to be as complicated as we have made it either. Here are a few ideas we have tried over the years in my family and in Husband's family to do things differently. These ideas try to alleviate one or more stresses related to gift giving: the pressure to choose the perfect gift, the unnecessary stuff we accumulate, and the money we spend. A few of these ideas try to help us focus outside ourselves completely. It can be good to give gifts, and it can also be good to rethink our gift giving to make it more purposeful, to recklessly love our neighbors.

Limit the number of gifts per person. The Savior of the world received three gifts around His second birthday. My sister limited her kids' gifts to four by incorporating "something you want, something you need, something to wear, something to read." Giving good things to our children does not mean giving all the things to them.

Draw names and choose a theme. Instead of buying gifts for everyone in Husband's family, we draw names (either individuals or couples) and give one themed gift. Themes we have done before include games, books, and shopping from thrift stores.

Give gift cards. It's almost completely thoughtless, but sometimes it's nice to give the gift of choice. My siblings and our parents contribute a bunch of gift cards, and we all play bingo to win them as prizes. We compete; we bond; we have fun. And nobody goes home with the same number of gift cards to fuel continued sibling rivalry.

Be present to give a present. You are not expected to buy a gift for an event you can't be present for. My siblings are more than welcome to roll their eyes at this one, as we almost never make it to my nieces' and nephews' birthday parties from out of town.

Give what you are able. We often collaborate to buy gifts for our parents. We don't try to contribute the same amount of money, but rather each person gives what he or she can according to his or her budget. Nobody complains or feels pressure to do otherwise.

Give experiences. My parents have often given experiences to the grandkids instead of gifts. Trips to a theme park, vacations at their cottage, memberships to the zoo, babysitting services so that Mommy and Daddy can go away for a weekend. We prefer gifts that create memories instead of clutter, gifts that will have a much bigger impact on their lives than a toy.

Intentionally match the gifts you give your family to your community. What says, "I love my neighbor as much as I love myself" more than choosing to give as much as you receive? This might mean filling a Christmas shoebox for a child in poverty around the world or having your kids pick out a gift to give to another child in need in your community. This could also mean sending extra money to your church's missionaries overseas to allow them a special splurge.

Give twofold. There are plenty of places to shop for stuff that will in turn support great causes and people. For example, Noonday Collection is a standout fashion company that empowers artisans living in poverty all over the globe. Or shop from people you know, like small business owners in your community or your mom friends who are trying to make a living from home selling cleaning products, skin care, and essential oils.

Give to a good cause. One year, in lieu of gifts, we decided as a family to donate money to Gospel for Asia, a mission organization that preaches the gospel to unreached people groups. We enjoyed the relief from giving one another gifts so much that we have never returned to the same volume of gift giving since.

The conversation with my family about gift giving took place in the middle of October; we hadn't even reached Thanksgiving, as if that ever stopped anyone from talking about Christmas. But part of me just wanted to dwell on the peace of that night in Bethlehem some two thousand years ago. Part of me wanted to feel that same peace and overwhelming joy of celebrating the time that God chose to come to earth in the flesh.

Part of me wanted to return to the simple yet profound message of Christ saying, *Remember that time I gave up everything so that I would be one step closer to saving you from the eternal destruction you were doomed for since birth? Remember, beyond the white noise and messes of tinsel, that silent and holy night I entered this world as an innocent, vulnerable baby?*

So much of that has been lost in the name of tradition, in the chaos and stress of planning the perfect parties with the perfect food and the perfect gifts. I don't want the reason I choose to forgo gift giving to be purely selfish, to be purely the case of a bad attitude. Any kind of giving requires a sacrifice of time or money or emotions. But I want to do it well, with purpose.

Child, remember. Remember that giving gifts is not all about you and yours, but about them and theirs too—those neighbors near and far who have needs much more imminent than your wants. Remember the birth of My Son was about My good news of great joy that is for all people.

Child, remember. A Savior has been born to you; He is Christ the Lord.

To Take This Deeper

Give Gifts

- **Reflect:** What kinds of attitudes are you instilling in yourself and your children about gifts? Does your attitude demonstrate that it is actually better to give than receive? Are there traditions that stress you out and keep you from enjoying the simple beauty of this holiday that originated in a stable with a few people, a couple animals, and a manger filled with hay?

- **Take Action:** Discuss as a family how you can focus not just inwardly on yourselves in your gift giving but on sharing Christ's love with your neighborhood, or those neighborhoods nearby that Christians like to avoid, or those neighborhoods around the world that are literally starving.

- **Read:** Read 1 Timothy 6:6–19. Don't be hindered by the constant search for more stuff. Find contentment in your basic needs and give generously.

Twenty-Four

Let There Be Peace at the Magic Tree House

Give Peace a Chance

Be united with other Christians. A
wall with loose bricks is not good. The
bricks must be cemented together.

—Corrie ten Boom[1]

The mall's play place is between Dick's Sporting Goods and Younkers and right next to the glorious aromas of Auntie Anne's pretzel booth. They call it the Magic Tree House. I love that name so much, as if the child protesting his mom's seven desperate minutes of shopping is enchantingly transformed the moment they enter the boundaries of the Magic Tree House.

And I'm pretty sure I love its nickname even more: the Germ Tree. Because that's exactly what it is: an organic, topical version of the flu virus.

Baby and I made our way through the mall of my child-hood memories to the Magic Tree House. My friend Aubrie and her two kids arrived soon after. While her son ran toward the slides and her daughter clung to her lap, Baby did her best to escape every time I wasn't looking. This scrambled our conversation, as did the standard chaos of head injuries and sweaty sock feet around us, but we rallied. We carefully opened bags of animal crackers and cereal, kind of–sort of pretending we didn't see the sign on the way in that clearly stated, "No food or drink within the play area."

After Baby attempted several more jailbreaks, I tried to rein her in from the great big world outside the Magic Tree House with a few toys I had brought along—her bright pink singing purse, complete with a pink bracelet, a blue credit card, a purple set of keys, and a pink touch-screen phone. And that's when war broke out; that's when Baby finally wanted to sit down on my lap and stay awhile. Because someone *else* wanted to play with her toys. Aubrie's daughter wanted to hold the bright pink purse, look inside the bright pink purse, and take a toy or two out of the bright pink purse. And Baby would not have it. She grabbed it away, Aubrie's daughter screamed, I gave the purse back, and we were left with the sounds of the apocalypse echoing around us.

Unfortunately there is no negotiating with children at this age. They can't be bribed, just distracted. They can't be talked off the ledge, just hugged tight. I said the word *share* over and over and was given the same angry eyes and mis-understanding tears that said, *Mine! All mine! Why are you letting her steal my stuff?!*

It didn't matter if I said things like, "It's nice to share, sweetie. Jesus wants us to share what we have, honey." No

Sunday-school answers would calm the storm of a one-year-old who didn't want to share her toys. Aubrie and I looked at each other. I'm pretty sure there was a speck of crazed hopelessness in each of our eyes over the weeping and gnashing of teeth coming from our distraught little girls.

"Why is it *so hard* for kids to learn to share?" we wondered aloud. And that's when the Lord cut through what had become the chaos of two tantruming children.

Isn't it interesting that children find it so difficult to share?

Why, yes, yes, it is. I find it quite interesting that sharing is the hardest social skill for children to learn. Because although we talk about it over and over growing up, and although we might make great strides to neither take other people's things nor hoard our own things to ourselves, we adults only pretend to be really good at sharing.

I know I pretend. I am big talk about how I don't value stuff more than people, but be prepared to receive a stiffly cold shoulder if you incorrectly handle my first-generation iPod Touch. Don't be surprised if you are shunned when you borrow my clothes without asking. And heaven forbid you eat that last Dove chocolate I saved for myself to indulge during Baby's naptime. In comparison to some, I might not have a lot of things, but that doesn't mean I am good at sharing what I do have. It doesn't matter how much I preach the message "Jesus wants us to share" over and over to Baby. At least, it doesn't matter if I don't set a good example for her.

> If I give all I possess to the poor and give over my body
> to hardship that I may boast, but do not have love, I gain
> nothing. (1 Cor. 13:3)

While at times I might struggle to selflessly share, I don't think I underestimate the importance of sharing. As our daughters were demonstrating so well that day, and as I have experienced other times in my life, conflict happens when we refuse to share. I have been tempted to oversimplistically state that all wars and world conflicts are the result of someone's selfishness, but true peace can never exist apart from Jesus, the Prince of Peace, no matter how much the world holds hands and learns to share. And if true peace is only found in Christ, that means there is only one place true peace can exist, which is the church: the body of believers who live with Christ in their hearts and are given command after command to live at peace with one another.

> Let the peace of Christ rule in your hearts, since as members of one body you were called to peace. And be thankful. (Col. 3:15)

Over the past twenty-four days I have thought about God urging me to share, give, show kindness, and reach out to the lost people of this world. I've thought about how our acts of love and compassion create opportunities to share the gospel. But through the apostle Paul, God also urges us to care for one another within the body:

> Therefore, as we have opportunity, let us do good to all people, especially to those who belong to the family of believers. (Gal. 6:10)

Ah, the sweet, sweet harmony of the body of believers. The beauty of a congregation that is unified to one another, gets along with one another, and shares with one another. Except that being unified, getting along with, and sharing become really hard to do, *especially* within the beloved body of believers.

I mean, am I the only person to ever think horrible thoughts about certain people at church simply because I do not like them? *Oh my goodness gracious, if my brother in Christ raises his hand one more time during this committee meeting, I will go all Chuck Norris on his grandma. And if my sister in Christ asks us to pray for her sick fish again, I will skeet-shoot that prayer request straight out of the sky. And her fish.* I mean, these kinds of people totally exist, right, even at church? *Especially* at church?

But peace and unity and sharing at church aren't difficult only because we don't like certain people in our congregations. Sometimes we let our trivial opinions and our desire for power take priority over sharing with others. We don't like to share in the sacrifice of our missionaries because that might mean there won't be room in the budget for centerpieces at the next church potluck. We don't like to share the stage of worship with others because they might use an instrument that doesn't fit our taste. We don't like to honestly share our hurts and temptations because then people would know we don't have it all together like we pretend to.

It's easy to see the church isn't perfect. It's easy to see that certain people and their personalities clash even with the curtains hanging up in the sanctuary. It's easy to see the body has found plenty of trivial *and* significant issues to argue about and work through and split over. But one of Christ's final, most desperate prayers on earth was for us as the church. He prayed for us to be unified so that the world would know God was the one who sent Him.

We have a lot to share within the body of Christ: wealth, power, time, resources, vulnerability, friendship, hospitality. Which means we also have a lot to keep to ourselves. But if we, as the church, share our lives with those people in the church who are difficult to love, we might better understand why they are the way they are. We might understand their hurts and heartaches and start to feel even the tiniest warmth of loving sympathy toward them. And if we, as the church, put our trivial opinions and hunger for power aside, we might better demonstrate how the church works best as a fully functioning body. We might expand beyond our close circles of friends and find that peace really does have a chance within our congregations.

Do you hear that, My child? Do you see the opportunity to be My light, simply by loving your brothers and sisters who are a part of My body? Do you realize that when you love those within the church, you are demonstrating to the whole world that you are My disciple?

Sharing, and all the things that word entails, is powerful. When we combine the humble act of sharing with Christ's grace, we not only proclaim that we are His disciples (John 13:35), but we proclaim the power of a God who is able to unify our bizarre, motley crew of saved sinners. We give peace a chance, at least where peace is possible before Christ's return.

I'd like to say that after our soothing, motherly voices whispered sermons into our daughters' ears, they recognized their sisterhood in Christ and chose to play in sweet, sweet harmony. But nope. They battled off and on the rest of our playdate, like an hour-long game of Cops and Hoarders as they mourned the fact that one bright pink singing purse could not be in two different little girls' hands at the same exact time.

We did not find much peace at the Magic Tree House, but the dreams of our daughters being future BFFs didn't wilt completely. We knew it would take years of preaching Sunday-school answers—or, more accurately, years of *demonstrating* the word *share*—before they learned why it's so important to live at peace with one another.

To Take This Deeper

Give Peace a Chance

- **Reflect:** What do you find difficult to share within the church: possessions, money, vulnerability, friendship? How can you demonstrate the importance of sharing to your children or other young people in your life? In what ways has sharing created peace among those around you?
- **Take Action:** Ask the council of your church if there are any needs that have been reported by other members. Consider what you are able to share to help meet one of those needs.
- **Read:** Read Colossians 3:8–17. Practice the kinds of qualities that create peace and unity among believers.

Control Enthusiast

Give Way

The secret of following God's will, I discovered, usually is wrapped up in rejecting the good for God's best.

—K. P. Yohannan, *Revolution in World Missions*[1]

I stood outside the bedroom door and prayed. *Begged* is more like it.

Sleep. Please sleep. I just want her to be healthy again. I just want her to get rid of this cold for good. I just want a break. Lord, please *make her fall asleep.*

Baby was fighting something nasty. Something that had made many special-guest appearances over the past month and wouldn't get lost for good. Something with way too much mucus clogging and pouring out of way too many places. Something that made her cling to Mommy all day and get way too little sleep at night. She was in her crib for an attempted nap, taking turns hacking, crying, and coming within inches of slumber, which is why I stood right outside the bedroom door, once again fiercely praying for even an hour of serenity.

Maybe it's silly to pray for stuff like that. I realize a mucusy cold and a missed nap will not be the hardest part of motherhood. If Baby becomes Toddler and then Kid and then Teenager someday, I'll be praying, *Thank You, Lord. Also, heaven help us work through back talk and missed curfews and menstruation.* But this stage of caring for small people was physically exhausting. It was to the point where it felt like a hundred red bolts of lightning were piercing my eye sockets at all hours of the day. It was to the point where Husband would look at me at 8:45 p.m. and say things like, "We're lots of fun when we're not tired." Meaning, we're *not* much fun.

Silly or not, small problem or not, sleep was what Baby needed to get healthy again. I continued to fervently pray, *Sleep. Please sleep. I just want her to get healthy again. I just want her to get rid of this cold for good. I just want a break. Lord,* please *make her sleep.*

Baby's coughs and cries quieted down, so I walked to the other bedroom, lay down on the bed, and turned on the baby monitor—a blessed reminder that I was never quite off duty. I stared at the monitor as if I were in a state of emergency, waiting for news of a bombing. I just wanted five solid minutes without lights blinking or noisy crying to feel assured she was actually sleeping. I just wanted to rest my eyes for five solid days.

But as I waited in anticipation to see what the outcome of my prayers would be, I felt God reminding me, *You may know what you want, but I know exactly what you need.*

When I am being completely honest and horribly disrespectful with a touch of overly tired, sometimes I wonder if that is true. Sometimes I wonder if God *really* knows what

I need. Sometimes I think God should *really* call my hotline and let me give Him a little advice on how to better run things down here. And after only a couple decades living life on earth, I know it is because I am a Control Enthusiast. Let me state that more clearly: control is my *idol*. I like to feel comfort in the pretense that within a certain percentage of my life, I call the shots. A control *freak*, if you will.

I have been this way a long time, trying to be in control, trying to make plans and stick to those plans as if they were taken straight out of Scripture. In kindergarten I planned to be a gymnastics teacher when I grew up. In fifth grade I planned my breasts would flower like all my friends' did. In high school I planned to go straight to the mission field after graduation. In college I planned (a few different times) whom I would marry. And in marriage I planned to wait at least two years before trying to have children.

Cute, said the Lord. *How about I make you tall enough to play volleyball instead? How about I give you size AA boobs, a college degree, and a baby earlier than you thought instead? And by the way, Justin Timberlake is already taken. How 'bout I bring "sexy back" through Husband instead?*

All those plans displayed the supposed control I had over my life. All those plans God ruined, replaced, and greatly improved with His ability to see the bigger picture I cannot.

> Many are the plans in a person's heart,
>> but it is the LORD's purpose that prevails. (Prov. 19:21)

I remember praying fervently for those requests. I remember thinking, *Lord, these are good things, so obviously You should say yes!* I remember learning it's really hard to honestly pray, *Thy will be done, Lord.* I pray for good things all the time: health, safety, financial security, happiness. I come up with such good things to pray for it's hard to understand why God would ever say no. But how often do I stop and pray, *More than anything I want,* Thy *will be done, Lord?*

> "Your kingdom come,
> your will be done
>   on earth as it is in heaven." (Matt. 6:10)

It's even harder for me to apply this prayer to parenting, to stop and pray, *More than anything I want for my child, Thy will be done, Lord. Even more than I want my child to be safe, even more than I want her to be healthy, even more than going to a good school with good opportunities and good chances to get into a good college. Even more than I want my child to find a good job and marry a good spouse and live in a good home and have good kids,* Thy will be done, Lord.

Even typing out those prayers makes me feel a mini panic attack inside my chest as I unclench my fingers and surrender my pretense of control, as I entrust our child into the Father's hands the way He entrusted her to ours in the first place. I want good things for Baby; loving parents want good things for their children. But Christian parents also want what's best for their children, *God's best* for their children. It's not that God's will never includes good things for us or for our kids. Even in this world of evil, sickness, and death, He creates good from bad. Even in our darkest nights He draws us closer to Him, shapes us to be more like Him, and carries us through as we cling tightly to Him. And that's what I pray for our child too: *Thy will be done, and please, Lord, let her know You.*

> Blessed is the one
>> who trusts in the LORD,
> who does not look to the proud,
>> to those who turn aside to false gods.
> Many, LORD my God,
>> are the wonders you have done,
>> the things you planned for us.
> None can compare with you;
>> were I to speak and tell of your deeds,
>> they would be too many to declare. (Ps. 40:4–5)

Most of the time I know what I want, but God *always* knows what I need. When I pray, *Thy will be done,* I yield to His purpose; I give way and let Him take the wheel. I watch my idol of control crumble before me into the fickle dust it was made of, that idol of control that only displays my lack of trust in the One who actually knows best, only demonstrates my inability to see He is taking care of me and has my best in mind. Moreover, it only shows my inability to see the bigger picture, that He has a redemptive purpose for the entire world.

> Teach me to do your will,
>> for you are my God;
> may your good Spirit
>> lead me on level ground. (Ps. 143:10)

If God asked me what I wanted today, I'd probably choose sandy beaches and handfuls of chocolate chips. I'd choose piles of books and lots of naps. I'd choose little contact with other human beings. I'd choose quiet, safe, and comfortable. Basically, I'd choose to take a vacation—something good. But sometimes

God doesn't ask, because He has something way better planned. He knows that life and its relationships and commitments and exhaustion and hardships are how we grow, how we are stretched, how we become a little more like Him each day.

You may know what you want, but I know exactly what you need.

I can be disrespectful. I can whine and beg and plead and pray for everything except "Thy will be done." I can think things like, *Easy for* You *to say, Lord!* But it wasn't easy for Him to say, was it? It wasn't easy for Him on that night His soul was "overwhelmed with sorrow to the point of death" (Matt. 26:38). He felt so much anguish, His "sweat was like drops of blood falling to the ground" (Luke 22:44). He knew exactly the physical, emotional, and spiritual torture He would face through betrayal, arrest, disownment, rejection, mockery, flogging, being nailed to the cross, and dying a death completely forsaken by God. Yet He knelt down and prayed, "My Father, if it is possible, may this cup be taken from me. Yet not as I will, but as you will" (Matt. 26:39).

Jesus, just hours before He would face the cruelest, most unfair pain, prayed that prayer. Once again, He set the perfect example for us. Once again, He was able to say, *I've been there, so let Me show you the way to surrender. Let Me lead you in a life that yields and gives way to God's "good, pleasing and perfect will"* (Rom. 12:2).

The coughing began again. Baby started to cry, and the lights flashing on the monitor told me naptime was over. A solid twenty-six minutes. That was how God answered my prayer. I was still tired; the few minutes of dozing didn't quite take away the feeling of a hundred red bolts of lightning piercing my eye sockets. But for the moment, that was okay.

Rejoice always, pray continually, give thanks in all circumstances; for this is God's will for you in Christ Jesus. (1 Thess. 5:16–18)

God knows exactly what I need. Which means He would provide the strength and grace and loving mercy I needed to fight through exhaustion for one more afternoon. God knows exactly what Baby needs too. Which today, as she fought through a stubborn cold, was a Mommy to offer extra loving snuggles.

Yes, child. You may know what you want, but I know exactly what you need. My will be done.

To Take This Deeper

Give Way

- **Reflect:** What areas of your life are hard to surrender to God? What things would you rather cling to than choose to pray, "Thy will be done"? It's okay to pray for what we want. Even Jesus, fully human and fully God, did that. But remember to follow His example, that even when we face the worst circumstances, we are taught to pray, "Thy will be done."
- **Take Action:** Be aware of the plans, circumstances, or desires God may be calling you to surrender to His will. It's always easier said than done, but rejecting what we think is good for what God knows is best is a beautiful act of putting our ultimate trust in Him.
- **Read:** Read James 4:1–10. Give way from friendship with the world and submit to God.

Twenty-Six

The Sidewalk of Motherhood

Give Life

In my opinion, if abortion is permitted in
wealthy countries that have all the means
that money can buy, those countries
are the poorest among the poor.

—Mother Teresa[1]

(This chapter includes my personal reflections, my sister's retelling of the day's events, as well as excerpts from Mary Verwys's book *Wednesday Mourning: A Sidewalk Counselor's Journal of God's Grace in the Abortion Struggle.* My sister volunteers as a sidewalk counselor at the abortion clinic in our hometown. Mary is her mentor and the director of Garden of Hope ministries, also in Grand Rapids, Michigan.)

My Sister

It was sunny outside. I watched as a young woman stepped out of her Jeep.

She was willing to talk to me right away, so I immediately offered her all the support our ministry provides. I asked her why she came here today and why she was alone. She was very open, telling me she is a college student and that she felt pressured by her parents to abort this baby. She seemed unsettled but also willing to listen.

I showed her the fetal model of her baby at eight weeks pregnant. She told me where she attended college, and I informed her of their incredible Students for Life group that would be willing to walk alongside her, even throw her a baby shower. She accepted my offer to go to the crisis pregnancy center just down the road.

Me

Just took a girl to (the crisis pregnancy center)—Pray, Pray, Pray!

That was the Lord's alarm that interrupted my superordinary morning via text message. We get these kinds of texts from my sister way too little. Most of the women she tenderly offers words of love and warning to choose to go inside and abort their babies anyway. The clinic she volunteers outside of is sixteen minutes away from where I was at my parents' house, just eating lunch and anticipating Baby's upcoming nap.

But a mere sixteen minutes away from my ordinary was a young woman facing a life-altering choice. Sixteen minutes was all that separated me from a young woman who woke up believing the only option for her future was to get rid of her unborn baby. I was only sixteen minutes away from this young woman and some of her emotions I wish I didn't relate to so well.

Mary Verwys

The abortion clinic that I counsel outside of has mostly middle and upper middle class people that use its services. I've seen BMWs, Jaguars, Cadillacs, and a host of other expensive vehicles. These women, of course, would need little of the help our ministry has to offer. They want for nothing. And apparently the one thing that threatens to undo their lives-as-they-want-it lifestyle, is the baby they're carrying. We all know women who sacrifice daily to care for their children. I am always shocked at a women's choice to abort when she can so easily afford to support her child very comfortably.[2]

Me

Husband and I had a plan. A plan to wait at least two years after we were married to try to have a baby. I remember staring at the positive pregnancy test just under a year earlier than we hoped to even start buying pregnancy tests. I remember typing a letter for Husband to break the news, and I remember him reading it. I remember him looking up to find me crying over the hot dogs I was frying on the stove for supper.

Dear Husband,

Right now I am a million different emotions at once. Right now I am nervous, excited, scared, and any other emotion that means I don't know what to feel. Let me explain. You are going to be a dad. I am going to be a mom. We are pregnant . . .

The tiny flare of excitement amid my million different emotions wore off pretty quickly.

The Plan. This baby wasn't part of the Plan.

My Sister

I offered to stay with the young woman at the crisis pregnancy center in case she didn't want to be alone, but she said she would be okay. I left her in good hands, as a dear friend of mine was working there that day. I also left her my number in case she needed anything.

Me

My letter to Husband continued:

> I am nervous: How are we going to pay for this? What are we going to do? Where are we going to live? How are we going to make it work? How? Why? Isn't it too soon?
>
> I am excited: There's a baby growing inside of me. It's half me and half you.
>
> I am scared: What if I miscarry? What if I do something to hurt our child? What if we aren't ready to be parents in nine months? What if we want more time with just the two of us? What if you are upset?

None of our circumstances were actually reasons to fear having a baby. Our budget would become tight, but not impossible. The only thing that would be inconvenienced by the birth of a baby was the Plan. But my own selfishness and idol of control were blinding. I battled dark emotions against what I viewed as the parasite overtaking my body, giving me cankles, and conniving how it would come out and ruin my life.

Then came the guilt. So many women were mourning their losses, waiting to be blessed with a baby. And on the other hand, so many women were giving in to the same feelings I was fighting. So many were darkening the door of that clinic just sixteen minutes from my parents' house, maybe now regretting their decision for a lifetime. But those were the women I related to: the ones who weren't thinking about the miracle growing inside of them, but about themselves and what they were losing in all of it. I started to understand the deception of control and freedom behind that decision.

Mary Verwys

Through the years on the sidewalk I think I have heard it all. I'm always interested in the reasons men and women give for making the decision to abort their child. . . .

Some point out the lies of a godless culture: It's my right to choose life or death. It's so small that it's not even a baby. It's better to abort the baby than give it up for adoption.

Some display an unbelievably selfish attitude: I don't want to lose my figure. I just started a new job, and don't want to give it up. I'm too young to be tied down.

Some put fear in my soul: I prayed about it and know it's God's will. This way God can just take care of it in Heaven. I know God will forgive me anyway.[3]

Me

I cried tears of joy when the doctor placed Baby in my arms for the first time.

But I soon realized that being pregnant with Baby was only the preliminary battle. Choosing to leave my beloved elementary teaching job and humbly accepting the task of stay-at-home mommy was an all-out war. It was my choice to stay home, but that just fed my I'm-a-martyr attitude. I felt like God asked me to do something holy called Teaching a Class of First Graders to Read, but then changed His mind and sentenced me to life in the Prison of Poopy Diapers, Dirty Dishes, and Stinky Laundry.

I missed my job, going out for dinner after seven o'clock with friends, and sleeping in with Husband past eight o'clock on Saturday mornings.

My Sister

A prayer request for the young woman was sent to our network of sidewalk counselors:

"Please pray for her tonight. If she chose life today, it would be very hard to continue in these next few months with no support. For her to go it alone will be scary. Please ask the Father with us to give her peace and softened hearts for those she needs to lean on. She had a 'bright future' all planned out, and her baby was not part of the picture. But as we have seen again and again, God can change all that!"

Me

It wasn't Baby's fault. As we were clearly warned our entire lives: first comes love, then comes marriage, then comes breaking the rules of your natural-birth-control methods during hot sex and a baby carriage.

But even as a woman who chose to physically give life to her child, there were still ways I chose to hike the Sidewalk of Motherhood grudgingly. Not slowing down to hold Baby's hand and gently walk at the pace she needed, but more like grabbing her arm and dragging her behind me as I worked toward whatever I thought was more important on my agenda.

She was too little to recognize it then, but if I had kept it up, she would have recognized it eventually. She would know. She wouldn't see a mommy who found joy in all circumstances, but a mommy who found only bitterness in the sacrifices the Sidewalk of Motherhood required.

As I thought about this young woman and prayed for her, and as it triggered memories of my own season of blind darkness entering motherhood, I felt God once again whispering into my soul:

You want to see the world through My eyes, but do you see your own child through My eyes? Do you see her not as some burden slowing down your real life but as the substance of your real life? Do you understand that the pursuit of My righteousness in whatever task I lay before you is more important than the pursuit of your own happiness?

Mary Verwys

As with our ancient sister Eve, having life our own way is too powerful a prospect for some to resist. I often think of that Garden of Eden experience. God Himself was Eve's Constant Companion. The world was perfect. She lived in blissful relationship with her husband. But still the allure of crafting the world *your* way on *your* terms proved too powerful to relinquish. And so it was with the young Christian teen. This young woman had plans. She had her future mapped out and nothing or no one would stand in her way.[4]

Me

My letter to Husband ended:

> Thankfully, I also feel a peace that passes all understanding, because even with all the above emotions, I know a few other things as well . . . God has always provided for us. God likes making our lives exciting. God wouldn't give us anything that we can't handle with His help. God knows and understands our futures. God gave us this baby.
>
> I love you. And even with all the uncertainty, I hope you can feel a twinge of excitement and happiness, just for tonight, before we freak out later about what this means for our lives.
>
> Your wifey

"Freaked out" was an understatement, but no, a baby too early for the Plan was not the *worst* thing that could ever happen to us. Because a million times yes, God gave us that baby.

My Sister

I posted on Facebook: "Seeing God so obviously at work is INCREDIBLE! Please be in prayer for [a young woman] who came to the abortion clinic this morning scared and alone. She left for a free ultrasound at the [crisis pregnancy center] without even entering the clinic for 'counseling' and an ultrasound. Please pray she chooses life! God and [our ministry] have her back if she does!"

Me

Lord, please be with this young woman. She is precious. Her baby is precious. In our culture suffering from so much blindness and evil, please help her choose the path that leads to life. Help this ministry surround her and support her through any financial or emotional burdens. They have her back if she chooses life, and because they are a ministry born of Your lavish grace, they have her back if she doesn't.

My Sister

Later this evening I messaged my friend to ask what happened. All she was allowed to say was this: "Praise God!"

Me

Motherhood is humbling. It's difficult. It's draining. It requires so much prayer, tons of patience, and all the grace.

But when the doctor said, "It's a girl." When she smiled at me for the first time. When she first said, "Mommy," and when I understood the gift of that title. When I finally realized that the Sidewalk of Motherhood is something to hike with joy. I knew God's best was better than I could have imagined.

Just burn the Plan.

To Take This Deeper

Give Life

- **Reflect:** Who has God placed in your life for you to care for that at times feels more like a burden slowing you down than an opportunity to show His love? Remember that the pursuit of God's righteousness in whatever task He lays before you is more important than the pursuit of your own happiness.
- **Take Action:** Choose joy. Work hard. Don't let the sacrifices you make on behalf of others give you an attitude of martyrdom. View people as the substance of your life, not the ball and chain holding you back. Pray for the women of our country to choose life, and for the rest of us to be there to love them whether they do or don't.
- **Read:** Read Philippians 2:1–18. Be inspired to do so many things: consider others better than yourselves, look to the interests of others, and do everything without complaining. Ugh. All the hard stuff.

Twenty-Seven

But Do They Deserve My Gift?

Give a Mouse a Cookie

People are illogical, unreasonable, and
self-centered. Love them anyway.
If you do good, people will accuse you of
selfish ulterior motives. Do good anyway. . . .
People really need help but may attack you
if you do help them. Help people anyway.
Give the world the best you have and
you'll get kicked in the teeth.
Give the world the best you have anyway.

—Dr. Kent M. Keith, from "The
Paradoxical Commandments"[1]

On the car ride home from an outing that night, I listened to
Other People talk about welfare. "Other People" as in white
conservative Christians, cut from the same kind of cloth I

was, talking about the United States' social welfare system. The end. That's today's whole story. And that was enough to make me run to bed and cry.

I knew these exaggerated emotions were just part of our transition back to the States, that these kinds of conversations about anything related to poverty were difficult to have after the sights, sounds, and smells of poverty were what we walked out our front door to every day for three years. And that's what bothered me about the conversation I had just listened to, not so much the politics of welfare as much as the complete disregard for how poverty is a lot more complicated than what we often reduce it to with politics.

Nobody mentioned that poverty is more complex than whether or not someone works for a steady paycheck. Nobody emphasized that he or she didn't know what it was like to be poor, or even mentioned anybody he or she knew personally who lived below the poverty line. Nobody recognized the great divide between the Uppers and Lowers of our society. Nobody talked about how maybe the church has also failed to do its part in caring for the Lowers at times. But everybody was about the word *deserve*, as in, "Do those people on welfare *deserve* what we are giving them?"

I appreciate having relationships with Other People who can get past the Kardashians to talk about things that matter, but I struggle listening to people say things that are way too easy for them to say. (Insert all the clichés about "pulling yourself up by your bootstraps" when your dad paid for everything you ever needed and wanted from age zero to eighteen, just like mine did.) It's *how* Other People talked about the issue. It's how all grace is obliterated when we focus on the oversimplified question, "Do they *deserve* what we are giving them?"

I have talked a lot about that stupid word, how sometimes we hesitate to give because we think *we* deserve something. But what I'm getting at here is that other times we hesitate to give because we think *the person we are giving to* is undeserving of our gift. The whole it's-not-me-it's-*you* kind of thing.

You are full of a lot of self-righteousness right now, My child. How easily you forget your battles with the exact same question not so long ago.

Ah yes. The reprimand from above that I needed to take a chill pill. The reminder that talking about complicated issues will never improve with rage and sass. The admonition that while it's good to be passionate, it's even better to be levelheaded and to maintain civility, peace, and unity with other Jesus People. Furthermore, the humbling rebuke I needed was that the question "Do they deserve my gift?" was something Husband and I had wrestled through often during our time in Guatemala, in various relationships with people in poverty.

I already talked about Pablino and Victoria, the elderly couple who lived right outside our school's fences. Our relationship with them was not just the helper and the helped, but a real friendship. Yes, spending time together took effort, mostly me fighting the "I'm Too Tireds" to visit them, but our relationship was a gift.

I haven't yet mentioned Victor, the man who sold freshly squeezed orange juice at our bus stop every morning. After learning enough Spanish to have a real conversation, we got to know Victor and his young son, Estuardo, a little better every school day. And as we got to know them better and a few times invited them over for meals, Victor began sharing about his hardships. We offered to help with finances as best as we could, both from our own paychecks and from funds that friends and family from the States had given us for situations like his.

At first, most of Victor's needs were related to medicine. He had had a brain tumor removed and still suffered from many symptoms that made it difficult for him to work unless he had the medicine he couldn't afford. But after a while it became a classic *If You Give a Mouse a Cookie* case study, where one request led to another, which led to another. Estuardo needed school supplies and a uniform. Victor wanted to buy an inventory of grapes to sell at Christmas to make extra income. His mother passed away, but his siblings refused to help pay for the funeral. He wanted to buy a piece of property that his mom still owed money on. He wanted to build a tiny house on that property. He was having heart surgery for his latest health issues.

It came to the point where we questioned whether Victor was telling the truth. He seemed so genuine, so kind, but could one man's life seriously be so crummy to have that many horrible things happen in a row? Could he possibly be using us as the rich white people from the United States who could be easily conned by their desire to be compassionate?

I digress as I introduce Alejandra, the woman who rang our doorbell the most. She always showed up with a baby tied to her back and a toddler holding her other hand, and we never got her story straight. One of the children was her nephew? Did she want a meal? A warm shower? Milk for the baby and money for medicine? The one time she accepted our invitation to come into our home, we realized our cell phone was missing after she left. We heard stories about her from friends. Was Alejandra only collecting money for her abusive boyfriend to pay rent? Was her name even Alejandra? We never knew.

We asked ourselves the same question over and over about Victor and Alejandra: Did they *deserve* our gifts? Were they using the money we gave them for what they said they needed it for, or was that money only supporting bad behavior and creating dependency on us? We didn't want to fund addictions, laziness, or abusive behavior; we wanted to be good stewards. Did we do the right thing? And the answer is, I don't know. The answer is, I don't have the answers.

But trying to answer the question "Do they deserve my gift?" created a lot of stress. It put a lot of pressure on us to be perfect Lie Detectors and Bad-Intention Radars. Sometimes I still feel a knot in my chest obsessing over whether we gave correctly. What if they weren't telling the truth that time we said, "Yes, we would love to support you"? What if they *were* telling the truth that time we said, "No, we will not give you money for that"?

I had a moment of clarity on a visit back to Guatemala just a few weeks ago. My friends and former coworkers and I were sitting around the table in the teachers' lounge at Inter-American School when we started talking about Victor: "He seems so kind and genuine, but is he really telling the truth when he asks for so much help? How can we be sure?" And then my friend Kylie shared this story:

> I worked in a coffee shop in Boston many years ago. One day a man called the store, saying he was in our coffee shop earlier and thought he lost his wallet and cell phone. We looked all over and couldn't find them anywhere. The man

was frantic, having just lost his ID, money, credit cards, and phone. He asked Ken, my boss, if he could do him a huge favor and lend him money to get back home. He needed enough for a bus and some food so that he could get his wallet and phone situation figured out. He promised to pay Ken back immediately. Ken really felt for this guy and wanted to help him out. The man stopped by the store and Ken generously gave him $150 from his own pocket.

Later that day, another café in our city's chain got the exact same phone call: a man had lost his wallet and phone and desperately needed some cash to get home. Ken was alerted to the second call and immediately knew he had been scammed.

I felt awful for Ken; he was an intuitive person and I know he didn't give to everyone who asked. I couldn't believe he had been so generous, and now was out $150! But immediately, without reservation, Ken said, "I would rather give if I believe someone is in need. If the other person feels the need to lie and manipulate someone, that is on them." If Ken felt in his heart he should give, he knew he was being true to God and himself, even if the other person wasn't. It was that simple for Ken.

When I asked Kylie for permission to share her story, she typed it in an e-mail and called it "Giving Like Grace." The final line of her message read, "The way that Ken gave taught me more about grace than I have ever learned before."

I don't have the answers to what we need to do about welfare. While they are related, I tend to think about the personal more than the political. And Washington, DC, is not who I ultimately answer to. But I do know one thing: Christ never asked the question, "But do they *deserve* My gift?" to the people He personally encountered. Not when He gave up heaven for humanity, not when He caused the blind to see and the lame to walk, not when He stood on the hills and preached His truth to the masses, not when He washed His disciples' feet, and not when He died in my place. He already knew I didn't deserve His gift. And yet that didn't hold Him back from giving me— an undeserving sinner—the gift of His grace.

> Very rarely will anyone die for a righteous person, though for a good person someone might possibly dare to die. But God demonstrates his own love for us in this: While we were still sinners, Christ died for us. (Rom. 5:7–8)

That fact makes me weep. Christ died for me, even though I didn't deserve it. Even though He knew I would take advantage of His gift of salvation each and every day. And that gives me freedom, freedom from the obsessive worry over giving "correctly." Husband and I prayed about supporting Victor and Alejandra. We asked God for wisdom, sought guidance from other Christians, and at different times we made different judgment calls. If Victor or Alejandra chose to take advantage of our compassion, that is not our fault. We did what we thought was right even if they chose, for whatever reason, to be dishonest with us.

Knowing Pablino, Victoria, Victor, Estuardo, and Alejandra changed the conversation on poverty for me. They reminded me that poverty is more complicated than what we read in textbooks and articles on the Internet. That I have no idea what it's like to be poor. That there is a great divide between the Uppers and the Lowers all over the world. That when I merely focus on whether or not a person deserves my gift, then I am part of the failure of the church to do its part in demonstrating Christ's boundless grace.

I've talked a lot about money, but it's not just people in poverty I ask this question about, is it? And it's not just money I worry about giving to others, is it? And Christ's example that voices the answer into my heart is not usually what I like to hear, is it?

"They're asking me for help, but they never paid me back last time!" *Give to them anyway.*

"She said that about me, and it really hurt!" *Forgive her anyway.*

"He annoys me so much I want to scratch out my eyeballs!" *Be kind to him anyway.*

Despised and rejected. Pierced for our transgressions and crushed for our iniquities. Oppressed and afflicted. But He gave anyway. Christ made absolutely no sense at all, did He? Grace makes absolutely no sense at all, does it?

To Take This Deeper

Give a Mouse a Cookie

- **Reflect:** Have you ever been taken advantage of by someone you tried to show kindness to? Have you ever made a tough judgment to give and worried about whether you did the right thing? Even if you were cheated in some way, remember that it is not your fault when someone else takes advantage of your compassion.

- **Take Action:** Are there people in your life who are tough to love? Maybe they don't take advantage of you, but they make you think all the time, *They don't* deserve *anything from me*. The next opportunity you have, choose to *give anyway*, whether it's eye contact, genuine conversation, forgiveness, or lending them a helping hand when they need it.
- **Read:** Read Luke 6:27–36. Remember that true grace, especially toward our enemies, makes zero sense in our world.

Open-Soul Surgery

Give Me Twenty

*Our desire to touch others must come from
the transforming power of Christ within.*

—Kristen Welch, *Rhinestone Jesus*[1]

This should be Day 1. I really wish this had been Day 1. But I'm not in charge of the timing of these things, so I'll just go with it.

It was Sunday, and it was our last day in Michigan. My sister and brother-in-law have six children, and today we watched Number Six get baptized. The service was beautiful. I had to hold back tears as I watched my sister's family gather around the baptismal bowl, because is there anything more stunning than a single family taking up half the church's stage as they present another life to Jesus? And then I had to wipe away tears as I watched my sister and her daughters sing, because is there anything sweeter than listening to children praise Jesus?

But I wish this had been Day 1 because of the sermon. It was not only one of those God used to gently whisper into my heart, but one where He might as well have taken a loudspeaker to my ears and shouted, *Listen! You really need to hear this!*

> Then he called the crowd to him along with his disciples and said: "Whoever wants to be my disciple must deny themselves and take up their cross and follow me. For whoever wants to save their life will lose it, but whoever loses their life for me and for the gospel will save it. What good is it for someone to gain the whole world, yet forfeit their soul?" (Mark 8:34–36)

The pastor compared losing our soul to Jesus and His gospel to surgery, to a strict diet, to consistent exercise. Because everyone loves surgery, strict dieting, and consistent exercise. #SarcasmFont

Deep down, I think there is a little "I want to be healthy" in everyone. Otherwise we wouldn't hog out on sweets for Thanksgiving and Christmas and then swear we are going to eat only celery starting January 2. It's just that very few are able to partner their "I want to be healthy" with the necessary diet and exercise. I mean, maybe I go three days before I swear the only thing that will keep me alive is to shove a cream-filled doughnut in my mouth to make it all feel better.

In the cheap Twinkie-and-Mountain-Dew country we live in, being healthy requires sacrifice, even surrendering to pain. Like the pain of saying, "Yes, I will wake up an hour earlier each morning to add a consistent workout to my daily routine." Or the pain of saying, "Yes, I will choose an apple over that cheesecake." And sometimes being healthy has less to do with food and exercise than it does with the sobering pain of saying, "Yes, I will sign up for surgery if that will save my life from cancer."

I have prayed for many things this month: *To maintain the joy of being Wife and Mommy amid the daily grind. To see the world through God's eyes. To live intentionally. To build relationships and share Christ's love with our neighbors. To learn what it really means to give. To collide motherhood with mission.* But the answers to my prayers start with something beyond physical health. Mike Yankoski explained in his book *Under the Overpass*:

> Jesus summarized right living in two powerful statements: "Love the Lord your God with all your heart . . . and love your neighbor as yourself." As over-spiritualized as it might sound, I really do think that caring for the needy begins with loving God more completely. . . . "Only in knowing God will we see people as they are, live as we were meant, and love as we were meant."[2]

If I want to be a person who embodies this prayer I have been praying, it starts here, on Day 28 but Should Be Day 1. If I want to be a person who lives joyfully, loves my neighbors, and thinks missionally, I have to start by loving God, and better yet, by letting Him love me first. By letting Him do His transforming work in me through what the pastor called "soul keeping." But if I'm being totally honest, surgery, diet, and exercise—even the spiritual, soul-keeping kinds—are not always high on my these-things-feel-awesome list. Because of the work, because of the pain.

I took notes during the sermon, mostly the questions I knew the Lord was yelling through His loudspeaker for me to ponder.

What are you holding on to that you don't want to let go of?

I ask God to perform open-soul surgery, to guide me toward a spiritually healthy life where I let go of things that pull me away from Him. But sometimes the choices I make are in complete conflict with that desire. Sometimes while I'm lying on the table praying for God to save my soul, I'm also twisting and turning my body away and batting at God's surgically steady hands. Sometimes I'd rather hold on to what I like to indulge in, even though I know it's as healthy for my soul as eating a stick of butter is healthy for my heart.

Scripture whispers, "Create in me a pure heart, O God, and renew a steadfast spirit within me" (Ps. 51:10).

But, Lord, I don't want to think about that before I go see the new R-rated comedy that will have way more f-bombs and male genitalia than I should ever care to partake in!

Scripture whispers, "With the tongue we praise our Lord and Father, and with it we curse human beings, who have been made in God's likeness. Out of the same mouth come praise and cursing. My brothers and sisters, this should not be" (James 3:9–10).

But, Lord, give me just a second to spread gossipy opinions about my friend's life choices.

Scripture whispers, "Now that you have purified your-selves by obeying the truth so that you have sincere love for each other, love one another deeply, from the heart" (1 Peter 1:22).

But, Lord, remember how I'm an introvert, so I'd rather only deeply love my Netflix account instead?

Scripture whispers, "But just as he who called you is holy, so be holy in all you do; for it is written: 'Be holy, because I am holy'" (1 Peter 1:15–16).

But, Lord . . .

Getting drunk. Flirting with someone who isn't my spouse. Laziness. Eating way more than I need. Loving my stuff more than God and others. Iniquities that not only affect my physical health and relationships but also my soul; that tear me away from God and from a healthy relationship with Him. Yes, the Christian life is about way more than avoiding the Big Sins, but that is still not a hall pass. The Bible is still clear.

What are you putting in that is hindering you from hearing My voice?

I know that what I shove into my mouth hole and how I use my muscles will affect the overall performance of my body, but eating healthy and getting exercise aren't natural desires of mine. Let me put it this way: when I was two years old, I was chubby and I was hungry. Whenever my parents opened the fridge, I came running; when we went to the pool, I stole food out of people's coolers; and I actually had a shirt that read *Feed Me*. Since then I lost my baby chub, but I never lost my appetite. I still feel the need to carb up for different activities, such as taking out the trash. And when someone says, "Drop and give me twenty," I want to reply, "How about I drop twenty reasons why we should hit up Pizza Hut instead?"

Spiritual diet and exercise often receive the same level of motivation from me. I think about my morning habit of waking up and immediately checking my phone: texts, e-mails, Facebook, and Instagram. My Google Calendar of to-dos. I think about our evening habit of plopping on the couch with the TV remote, ready to mindlessly watch whatever is on our TV channels or browse Netflix for hours, indecisively watching nothing. I think about how when I sit on the couch watching our TV, I can look out the window and see our neighbor's TV shining through his window fifty yards away, and how that feels a little bit like rotting.

I often feel hungry, but how often do I cultivate and satisfy a hunger for Scripture? I often claim I'm too busy to exercise, but how often do I overcome busyness for the sake of binge watching? After the name "Jesus," "Read your Bible and pray every day" is the second answer you have to be able to regurgitate in order to graduate Christian Childhood, but knowing an answer is much different than putting that answer into practice. As a wise woman told me, "We are commanded to go to the nations and make disciples. We cannot do that if we ourselves are not disciples, students of the Word."

Yes, God speaks to us through our circumstances, through our prayers, and through other people in our lives, but even when His voice seems distant or even mute in those ways, He always speaks in Scripture. We have an entire book of God's life-giving, soul-reviving words ready and available at all points of the day to read and meditate and wonder about. But I like junk food a little too much, completely out of moderation.

> My son, pay attention to what I say;
>> turn your ear to my words.
> Do not let them out of your sight,
>> keep them within your heart;
> for they are life to those who find them
>> and health to one's whole body. (Prov. 4:20–22)

I can claim to hear God's gentle whispers all the day long, but if Scripture doesn't back up what I claim to hear, then it's not actually God speaking to me. The deceitful whispers of decay and rust and temptation often feel more alluring than God's words of truth, His voice calling me back to Him.

My child, it's not about yesterday's failure. It's about today's faithfulness and obedience.

My OCD personality is prone to legalism in many areas of life, except diet and exercise of course. I'm prone to falling for claims like, "Do this and do that, and if you don't, feel really rotten about yourself forever and always." But that's why today I soaked up this passage from Hebrews, beckoning me to simply draw near to God, covered in His sweet-honey grace.

> Let us draw near to God with a sincere heart and with the full assurance that faith brings, having our hearts sprinkled to cleanse us from a guilty conscience and having our bodies washed with pure water. (Heb. 10:22)

Jesus said that our spirit is willing but our flesh is weak. Open-soul surgery means more than creating a list of great resolutions and our own willpower. Being spiritually mature does not mean being self-sufficient, but it means praying, *Lead us not into temptation* and finding complete dependency on God. It means drawing near to God in faith and obedience, and letting God cut out what is harmful to my soul.

It means listening for those questions that God often yells through His loudspeaker at me but I often ignore in the name of my own comfort or entertainment. Questions like, *What are you holding on to that you don't want to let go of? What are you putting in that is hindering you from hearing My voice? So much, Lord, I admit. Often, so much.*

To Take This Deeper

Give Me Twenty

- **Reflect:** How do you draw close to God so that He can draw close to you and transform your mind? How are you letting go of yesterday's failures and focusing on today's faithfulness and obedience? Ministry starts here. It starts by getting to know God and letting Him work in you first.

- **Take Action:** Something tells me that you know what action you should take. Is it to stop watching a certain show that fills your mind with junk? Is it to "unfriend" or "unfollow" someone who tempts you away from your spouse? Is it to stop, rest, and make time for Scripture?

- **Read:** Read Mark 7:1–23. Do not only honor God with your lips but with your whole heart. Let God perform soul surgery to rid your life of what makes a man "unclean."

Twenty-Nine

Where's the Sex, Drugs, and Rock and Roll?

Give the Gospel

*We're told to go and make disciples, but
we often just sit and make excuses.*

—Francis Chan[1]

We were back home in Illinois.

I guess all good things must come to an end, and I guess that meant I had to get back to running my own home and cooking my own food and paying quarters to wash my own laundry. #Sigh #MoochNoMore

I began by cleaning the windows, slider door, and bathroom mirror. While the paper towel in my hand swabbed up dirt and glass cleaner, my mind wandered back to a conversation I'd had with my grandpa the day before. We were sharing a meal after the baptism of my sister's Number Six when Grandpa asked me how our search for a new church in our new city was going. I unloaded a few of the reasons we thought it was hard to find a congregation to join.

"They weren't welcoming at all . . . There was so much unnecessary fluff . . . Their calendars were full of programs, but nobody seemed concerned with outreach . . ."

My last statement seemed to get Grandpa's attention the most. And the wise words of Jesus he said next were keeping my mind company as I did chores that day: "You know, it's not the pastor's job to make the congregation walk out the church's doors and share the gospel. The people need to do that themselves."

I agreed. That whole "A pastor can lead a congregation of horses to water on Sunday but can't make them share the water on Monday" thing.

Grandpa went on, "Do we have a Savior worth talking about? Because if we do, we should be talking about Him!"

Blast. Those weren't even empty words coming from him.

Everywhere my grandparents took us as kids, Grandpa had a natural way of bringing Jesus into the conversation. With us, with waitresses at the restaurants we ate at, with cashiers at the toy stores we dragged them to. It wasn't forced or awkward. Grandpa was simply so fascinated with Jesus and so grateful for what He had done in his life, it was like he couldn't help but talk about Him. It was like he cared so deeply for the random people we ran into, he never worried whether they would kindly smile at his Jesus words, or uneasily shy away, or coldly reject him. He was a natural Jesus Sharer.

When all the glass in our apartment was sparkling, I moved on to scrubbing the bathroom.

I can count on one hand the number of times I have explicitly shared the gospel with someone or made an effort to talk about Jesus to people I knew weren't Christians. Once in middle school when I invited my neighbor to youth group. Once in high school when I said I would "pray about it" to a college volleyball coach offering me a scholarship. His sarcastic response was, "Well, how do you know what the Lord will tell you?"

I have conflicting thoughts about all this. On the one hand, I believe a life lived above reproach can point others toward Jesus: Why are you respectful to our boss when he's such an idiot? Why do you stay married if your spouse is unpleasant to be around most of the time? Why don't you take part in rampant sex like the rest of us? Why don't you just stay home and celebrate a hangover on Sunday morning instead? Why do you associate with those lowlifes? Why aren't you obsessed with your 401(k)? Why do you feel peace when that part of your life is in shambles?

People might respond with fascination or wonder or maybe scoffing too. But the idea is that living healthy, hardworking, purposeful, generous, compassionate, and—most of all—hope-filled lives is already a bright light in the darkness.

On the other hand, I think that never sharing the actual words of the gospel with someone can also be like an airplane that takes off, soars high above the clouds, and circles around the airport but never lands at its tropical-paradise destination. It's simply missing a major point. And as cool as flying high in the sky can be, people need the hope of sandy white beaches and warm sunshine beyond the long, cold winter of this world we are living in. Beyond the hell of eternal separation from God we're headed toward otherwise, once the plane eventually runs out of gas.

A lot of people are nice. A lot of people are healthy and

hardworking and believe there is a purpose behind their choices in life. But hope, the kind that comes from Jesus, the kind that doesn't come from just anywhere, the kind that is only found in Him—that's what so many are lacking.

> Jesus answered, "I am the way and the truth and the life. No one comes to the Father except through me." (John 14:6)

People need to hear that Name. Whether they accept or reject that Name, they need to be introduced. But as I've mentioned before, I like to make excuses why I shouldn't share Jesus with others. I'm introverted. I don't want to make other people feel uncomfortable. I'm busy. I'm tired. I don't have a personal Jesus Story worth sharing.

That last one is what I was thinking about that day especially, that I don't have a personal Jesus Story worth sharing. The one I shared at my Profession of Faith in eighth grade was the same one shared by 96 percent of the kids at my church.

"I was raised in a Christian home, went to a Christian school, and attended church every Sunday." (Extra credit if you could say "twice" every Sunday.) "I went to Sunday school, youth group, and to (insert: third-world country) on a mission trip. I don't really know when I became a Christian. I have known Jesus my whole life. The end."

I guess that happens when you grow up in a city nick-named the Mecca of Reformed Christians. But it feels boring, boring like squirting blue cleaner into our toilet bowl on a Monday morning. Boring like scrubbing the toilet bowl with a prickly wand. Boring, as in, how will my story ever excite someone else to believe in Jesus? ("Come on! Spice it up a little! Where are the pre-Jesus crazy years? Where's the sex, drugs, and rock and roll? Where's the 180 turn to Choir Girl? Make us weep! Make us run to the altar and fall on our knees because of how you've changed your life around!")

"It's all about what Christ has done in your life," Grandpa said the day before. "If He has done great things for you, then talk about it!"

What he meant was, my personal Jesus Story isn't about *me*. That's my spoiled, entitled, privileged self's tendency, to think it's about me. To think that sharing *my* Jesus Story means sharing all the things *I* have done and all the ways *I* will try to be a better person. Airing all of *my* dirty laundry, as well as all the sins other people have committed against *me*—like an intimate Facebook status or something.

But nope, Grandpa nailed it.

> For Christ did not send me to baptize, but to preach the gospel—not with wisdom and eloquence, lest the cross of Christ be emptied of its power. (1 Cor. 1:17)

What makes my Jesus Story worth sharing is nothing I have done. What makes my Jesus Story worth sharing is that I was stained like a baby's onesie after a huge poopy blowout, and Jesus made me fresh-from-the-package stain-free; I was scummy like an ungreased casserole dish, but God put in the back work to scrub me clean. Or the less adorable version: I was on death row and condemned to hell for all my wrongs, but Jesus unlocked my cell door, broke loose my chains, and said, *I will take your place. You are free. I love you.*

And the details of that story are absolutely wild. Those juicy tidbits might not make my listener weep and run to the altar, but they have done me in more than once in my life.

As I share my Jesus Story, you might hear something like, "I was raised in a Christian home by loving parents who gave me every opportunity to hear the gospel." And then comes Christ: *But let Me tell you all about how I turned that knowledge into a personal relationship built on more than your parents' commitment to Me.*

I might also say, "My youth didn't involve sex, drugs, or much rock and roll besides Aerosmith." And Christ adds, *But let Me remind you how your nature is to worship an idol called Control Freak, and how I faithfully draw you back into My loving arms, over and over.*

I might continue with, "My Christian upbringing in a generally Christian community seems predictable." And then Christ says, *But let Me tell you about all the plans you have made that I have ruined and replaced with even better ones.*

I might slip in, "Sometimes I feel like I'm not good enough to be used by God for His kingdom work; it's draining and intimidating to be an introvert in an extoverted world." And then Christ butts in, *But don't forget that I created you, that I love you. Don't forget that regardless of your qualities I call you to recklessly love others without fear, and that I will equip you with courage and support to do exactly that if you just trust in Me.*

And as I finally get the picture that my story isn't actually about me, I will declare, "Let me tell you how the Holy Spirit brought me places that taught me to weep for the world as God does. Let me tell you how God transformed my soul through every dark place and broken heart. Let me tell you how Jesus gave me hope beyond everything we can see here. Let me tell you how I keep learning that my life and my small story aren't about me at all but are part of God's bigger story and redemptive plan for this world."

Yes, I did all of that, and I am doing all of that. I love you.
Then the kitchen timer went off, reminding me to gather the laundry from downstairs. I unloaded the bag of warm, clean clothes into a pile on the living room floor. I folded and stacked each article of clothing while Baby morphed into a tornado and destroyed it all.

> How, then, can they call on the one they have not believed in? And how can they believe in the one of whom they have not heard? And how can they hear without someone preaching to them? And how can anyone preach unless they are sent? (Rom. 10:14–15)

People who don't want you to leave the country point out that there's a mission field right here in the United States. And that is true; the lost are everywhere. So now that we are back in the United States, I don't want to neglect the mission field that is right here around me. I want to believe I live where I do for a reason, to share Jesus with the people who live right next to me, work right next to me, are on a path to eternal destruction right next to me. Because what if, beyond the excuses and halfhearted prayers for my neighbors to know Jesus, I earnestly prayed for, recognized, and intentionally pursued doors God opened to share Jesus with others? What if I trusted Him for the right words? What if I let my passion for Christ's grace overflow with its good news to my neighbors?

> And pray for us, too, that God may open a door for our message, so that we may proclaim the mystery of Christ, for which I am in chains. Pray that I may proclaim it clearly, as I should. Be wise in the way you act toward outsiders; make the most of every opportunity. (Col. 4:3–5)

Of course, this part of Christian work and faith and duty makes me nervous, makes my hands feel clammy. It makes me wonder how God could ever speak through me, how the heck an unbeliever could ever hear past all my awkward mumbo jumbo.

Lord, please open doors for me to share the gospel with people in my life who need to hear it. And please give me courage and clarity to share Your Name when the opportunity arises. And please help me get comfortable with stuff that makes me feel uncomfortable. And help me remember all the work beyond that is Yours.

I picked up my phone and called Joan. She invited us over for lunch the next day.

To Take This Deeper

Give the Gospel

- **Reflect:** Are there people in your life who still need to be introduced to Jesus, who would benefit from hearing your Jesus Story? Remember that your Jesus Story is not about you but about what Jesus has already done for you and through you in your life.
- **Take Action:** Pray for God to open doors to share the gospel with others, and for you to recognize open doors. Full of Christ's love within you and full of Christ's love for others, walk through those open doors.
- **Read:** Read Acts 2:14–41. Like the disciples, let the amazing details of Christ's life, death, and resurrection overwhelm you with joy, hope, and amazement.

Thirty

Too Early for a
Pregnancy Test

Give Patiently

*Faith helps us distinguish the path of obedience
from the drivenness of performance.*

—John B. Hayes, *Sub-merge*[1]

I warned you in the introduction this wasn't a success story.
And that is partially why I hated writing this chapter.

I was hoping to write about how through friendship and
prayer and the flawless sharing of my Jesus Story with Joan,
she became a Christian. That at our lunch that day we fervently prayed and sweetly embraced and cried happy tears as
the angels in heaven rejoiced over one more lost soul being
found. What a perfectly tidy end to this thirty-day journey
that would have been.

I had called Joan the afternoon before to see how she was
doing. I was hoping to get together with her, too, to recognize

an open door I had been praying for. After all of my yakking about sharing Christ's love with my neighbors, I wanted to put the gospel where my mouth is.

From that phone call until our scheduled gathering, I went through all the stages of freaking out: *Lord, I'm nervous to the point of nausea. Is this the open door I have been praying for? And if it is, what do I even say? Do I write a speech? Give her a Bible? Create an organized thirty-minute PowerPoint presentation to ensure the gospel is clearly and thoroughly communicated? Do I abandon ship and just post a Jesus meme on her Facebook wall?!*

Even after spending the previous morning reflecting on the conversation I'd had with my grandpa, it was hard to keep the pressure off myself: the pressure to create an opportunity, the pressure to share the perfect words, the pressure to *make her listen and repent.*

My child, those aren't your pressures to bear. I AM enough.

Baby and I went downstairs and knocked on Joan's door. She greeted us with a welcoming smile as the warm fragrance of chicken noodle soup wafted toward us from her kitchen. All through lunch I did my best to pay attention, both to what Joan was sharing as well as any opportunities to bring up Jesus. And then Joan asked me about our trip to Michigan.

"It was nice . . . lots of family time . . . saw a few friends . . . nephew's baptism . . ."

Boom. Church was in the conversation. Naturally. I had been thoughtlessly fidgeting with my soup as I retold our trip to Michigan, but now that the Lord's open door smacked me in the face, I nervously sloshed my spoon through noodles, carrots, and chunks of chicken as though I were a maniac. This was it; this was clearly an opportunity. Maybe not to give a thorough thirty-minute presentation of the Gospels of

Matthew, Mark, Luke, and John. Maybe not to get all up in Joan's grill and demand, "So do you want to ask Jesus into your heart? *Do ya?!*" But I knew it was some sort of something. I just needed the courage to walk through and see what was on the other side.

"So . . . um . . . Joan . . . do you go to church at all?"

"What did you say?"

(*Of all the times for my voice to waver and her hearing to fail. Honestly, Lord?*)

"Um . . . I said, 'Do you go to church at all?'"

And then Joan told me all about the church she attends. For more than a minute, for more than what a person can say if he or she goes to services only on Christmas and Easter. She talked about the priest at her church whose sermons she loves to listen to. She talked about which pew she usually sits in. I couldn't believe it. I mean, I *could* believe Joan went to church. I *couldn't* believe I had spent so much time and energy and tummy butterflies being nervous to tell someone about Jesus who was already a Jesus Person.

I said to Joan, "Well, I was going to tell you all about Jesus, but it sounds like you already know Him!"

"Oh yeah, I know all about Him" was her reply.

"How did you decide to become a Christian?"

"I was born Catholic. My mother was Irish." She was raised in the faith. Go figure. So was I. I might have grown up in the Mecca of Reformed Christians, but right now, in the South Side of Chicago, we were living in the Mecca of Irish Catholics.

And that is why I partially hated writing this chapter. I had really good intentions going into this lunch. I care about Joan; I love her and want her to have the same hope in Jesus

I do; I want her to have heaven. So I didn't want to wait until *never* to talk to her about this stuff. But hearing that Joan was already a Christian suddenly brought to light some of the bad intentions I didn't realize were hiding way deep down in the ugly spaces.

There was this twinge of me that felt disappointed. *Disappointed*, of all things. Not a "Yay, Joan! Do you realize what this means? You and I have this huge thing in common! We have Jesus! And we get to be with Him forever!" Nope. Disappointment, like I wish she wouldn't have been a Christian already so that *I* could have the ego boost of feeling like *I* had led her to Christ. Like *I* was partially doing the work with hopes of the Evangelist Badge of Honor *I* could get out of it. Not for the Lord's glory, not for the sake of the gospel, but for *me*.

I felt that since there wasn't a big U-turn toward Jesus that day, this was all a failure: my friendship with Joan, my efforts to share company with her, my concern for her eternity.

Goodness, I'm messed up.

Are You getting this, Lord? I am messed up.

But my "messed up-ness" didn't end there. After lunch with Joan, I carried Baby back upstairs to our apartment. And that's when the urge suddenly hit me.

Filled with my disappointment that had turned to a little unrighteous rage, I took a pregnancy test. If the morning wasn't going to be filled with the good news and angels rejoicing, I was hoping my afternoon would be filled with a different kind of good news and storks delivering.

Husband and I were trying to have another baby. It was one of those adorable situations where we said stuff to each other like, "Hey, let's just stop preventing," but in my head it was never just a go-with-the-period-flow kind of thing. I *really* wanted to have another baby.

Here's what was not strange: taking a pregnancy test when you are trying to have a baby.

Here's what *was* strange: taking a pregnancy test only two days after you have done the deed involved in trying to have a baby.

It was too early for a pregnancy test, but I was too stubborn and disappointed and obviously just plain too stupid to care. I wanted to know *now*. So I peed in a plastic cup. I used the dropper to extract urine from the cup. I squeezed four drops of urine out of the dropper and onto the pregnancy test. (Dumb dollar-store tests.) I waited and watched the whole two minutes as the test revealed the answer I already knew it would: *negative*.

Sitting on the toilet next to a plastic cup of my urine, the dropper, and the pregnancy test with only one pink line, I broke down and cried. I was finally coming back into my right mind, out of my morning's Savior Complex, out of my afternoon's intense impatience for life to happen. And it left me feeling exactly that: *broken*. But right there, right then, sitting on that toilet next to my urine and pregnancy test, *broken* is exactly what I needed to be. Because even with all my good hopes and dreams and intentions of getting to know our neighbors, recklessly loving our neighbors, and being the light of the gospel to our neighbors, I knew there was still a battle being fought inside of me, and *broken* was the only way to bring that battle to light. *Broken* was what it took to finally hear what God was trying to show me that day:

My child, those aren't your pressures to bear. I AM enough. Choose faithful obedience.

I need to be continually broken of pride and selfish ambition. I need to be continually broken and reminded that all on His own, without my "help," Christ is *enough*. Enough for me, enough for Joan, enough for anyone lost and seeking to find Him. I need to be reminded that the only thing up to me each day is choosing faithful obedience to God's commands. I need to be reminded that the Lord is so much grander and more mysterious and awesome than any limited thirty-day journey I can concoct on my own.

But like the culture I contribute to, I vote for instant gratification. Or any gratification that is guaranteed an end date. Jillian Michaels's "30 Day Shred"? Sign me up. The "Whole30" diet? Sure, why not? November's "30 Days of Social Media Gratitude"? I think my fingertips can handle that. I can do almost *anything* for thirty days, knowing there's an end in sight and maybe a few guaranteed-to-be-good results.

But, Lord, You want me to be willing to sign up for a lifetime of service that has no end date except death and no guaranteed results except glorifying God and becoming more like Jesus? You want me to do a lifetime of hard things like loving my neighbor, forgiving that jerk seventy times seven times, and following You wherever You say go for zero kinds of personal applause? You simply want me to choose faithful obedience each and every day?

> "So you also, when you have done everything you were told to do, should say, 'We are unworthy servants; we have only done our duty.'" (Luke 17:10)

God does things we can't understand sometimes. He lets us wait. He takes His time to work in us. He sometimes even brings us to the point of *broken* so that He can draw us back to Him, to better equip us to take part in His work, even though He doesn't need us.

> For it is God who works in you to will and to act in order
> to fulfill his good purpose. (Phil. 2:13)

This story, this month of my life wasn't supposed to be about guaranteed results, wasn't supposed to end with a pile of success stories. It was about being the light of Christ in everyday situations even when I didn't know the outcome. About letting God do His work through me, but also about letting Him do His work *in* me. About hearing His gentle whispers of "I love you," often where I least anticipated them. About loving others recklessly, despite being a person who does very little in life that is reckless.

This month was about learning that the good, slow work of God often takes time. Giving takes time. Relationships take time. Listening for God to speak and answer our prayers takes time. Change takes time, sometimes longer than I'd like. Longer than a weeklong mission trip or a twenty-minute speech at a school assembly. Longer than a thirty-day challenge. Beyond what I am able to do on my own. Beyond who I am able to be without God's grace and mercy.

> Therefore we do not lose heart. Though outwardly we are
> wasting away, yet inwardly we are being renewed day by
> day. (2 Cor. 4:16)

But there is value in the waiting, in being patient enough to see where God takes you. There is value in the trusting and hoping. Am I willing to go all in, for a *lifetime* of work? Am I willing to take small steps of faith, each and every day, without knowing whether everything will end up happily ever after on earth or labeled "successful" in the world's eyes? Knowing the work I do is not for me, but is an act of worship to my Creator?

> Not to us, LORD, not to us
>> but to your name be the glory,
>>> because of your love and faithfulness. (Ps. 115:1)

Am I willing to wait to take another pregnancy test, knowing it still might not give me the answer I am praying for? Am I willing to keep praying anyway? To let God continue to teach me, show me, what it means to recklessly love my neighbor?

Yes, Lord. Cover me with Your sweet grace and send me forward. I will go. And when necessary, I will wait.

> Let us not become weary in doing good, for at the proper
> time we will reap a harvest if we do not give up. (Gal. 6:9)

To Take This Deeper

Give Patiently

- **Reflect:** What are you waiting for to happen in your life or in the lives of others around you? What is God teaching you while you're in the waiting room? Remember that God is bigger, more awesome, and more mysterious than any thirty-day challenge we could ever try to limit Him to.

- **Take Action:** Pray for endurance to love God and love your neighbor. Be content to take part in the good, slow, redemptive work of God in this broken world. Choose faithful obedience each and every day.
- **Read:** Read Colossians 1:3–14. Know that God's glorious might can strengthen you with endurance and patience in order to live a life that bears fruit in every good work.

And Since Then?

Happy are they who know that discipleship
simply means the life which springs from grace,
and that grace simply means discipleship.

—Dietrich Bonhoeffer, *The Cost of Discipleship*[1]

I took another pregnancy test a week later. It came back positive.
But so did the genetic test for triploidy after our baby died in
my womb at thirty-three weeks. We named her Aliza Joyce.
And that's probably the shortest possible way to tell you about
the longest, darkest year of our lives so far.

I set these thirty days of stories and reflections aside
through my pregnancy and the first months of grief. When
I came back to them, I wondered if I would even care
anymore. After months of either severe pain or intense
numbness in my heart, would I even care about all the
things I had learned and thought about on that thirty-day
journey? Listening for God to say, "I love you" throughout my day? Learning what it means to recklessly love my
neighbor? *Cute*, I thought. *I've barely been able to get off the
couch for the past few months.*

But I did care. With the deepened perspective that death
gifts those it leaves behind, I cared even more. If our time in
Guatemala taught me there's more to life than the pursuit of

my own happiness, the death of our daughter taught me the profound compassion of loving other people within their own stories of pain, grace, and hope.

I could go on and on about the kindness we were shown during this time of sorrow: from the congregation we eventually joined and love with our whole hearts; from family; from friends, old and new. I could go on and on about how just as there are times to give and love with reckless abandon, there are also times to humbly accept and receive.

We chose the name Aliza because it means "joy" or "joyful." It became a symbol of our grief, learning to choose joy in any and all circumstances. And I keep learning from her name, especially as God continues to teach us that truly loving others is best motivated *not* by formulating a bunch of man-made rules for ourselves, *not* by constant guilt over what doesn't come naturally, but by the deep joy of accepting Christ's great love for us.

> Enjoy serving the LORD,
>> and he will give you whatever you ask for.
> Depend on the LORD.
>> Trust in him, and he will help you.
> He will make it as clear as day that you are right.
>> Everyone will see that you are being fair. (Ps. 37:4–6 ERV)

My favorite example of this was when someone new moved to our apartment building. We decided to welcome him with a gift card for dinner out, just like Jim did when we moved in. Our new neighbor was so grateful, insisting he repay us with some sort of favor. It felt so awesome to be able to shake our heads, smile, and say, "Don't worry about it.

Someone did the exact same thing for us." The perfect "We love because He first loved us" kind of thing.

Oh, I have made plenty of mistakes. Reckless love became thoughtless love more than I wish to admit, like that one time I tried to serve our Muslim neighbor two slices of sausage pizza, or like that other time I invited our neighbor to church and didn't follow up before he moved away a month later. But we have also enjoyed some beautiful moments with the people we've shared our lives with: celebrating birthdays and a wedding, eating takeout and ice cream around our dinner table, squashing chairs and bodies into our small living room to watch the Super Bowl. Having conversations about heaven and hell with people you know feel lost.

But almost two years have passed since these thirty days of stories and reflections, and guess what? I'm still an introvert. I know, because just one month ago I discovered that wearing sunglasses makes it 80 percent more comfortable to sustain eye contact with other people, and that made my heart rejoice in song. I still need to recharge, still need quiet. But moreover, if I want to love the everyday people in my life without depending on my limited energy and skill, if I want to save my heart from dying a horrible death that leaves me an embittered Christian who can't understand why I only feel hatred toward loving other people, then I need *Christ* in the quiet. I need His words, the rejuvenating truth of the gospel.

No matter our personality traits, no matter if our love for others is rooted in the deep joy of Christ's love for us, that still doesn't make the work easy. There is a beautiful tension to be found between believing in a gospel that completely wrecks a lot of things we have become too comfortable with in this world, and finding peace in both who we are and who Christ is working in us to help us become. I'm at peace with being an introvert, and I'm at peace with the fact that Christ calls me to a reckless kind of love that will at times make my hands feel clammy.

Especially today, I think about how this simple command isn't easy, as I stare at boxes of stuff I packed for our next move. Another new job, another new city: Milwaukee this time. After two years of getting established in the South Side of Chicago, making friends and finding a church and recklessly taping invitations to our neighbors' doors each month, we are approaching another season of starting over. Nope, it's never easy.

But what a delight. Beyond the exhaustion of the logistics behind another move and the deep ache of leaving people we love, what a delight to follow where God leads. What a delight to feel God's "I love yous" when He says, *See, I have given you this desire in your heart. Follow Me on the path that will take you there.*

And what a delight to continue to pray, *Lord, let us learn to recklessly love our neighbors no matter where, no matter when, no matter what.* It's never easy, but what a delight.

So we remember that our identity is in Christ, regardless of our personality traits. We accept God's epic grace for ourselves and let that grace overflow to others. We continue to ask ourselves hard questions and pray scary prayers. We work for His glory alone. Every single day.

Lead us, guide us along the way, Lord. Give us Your strength.

With this in mind, we constantly pray for you, that our God may make you worthy of his calling, and that by his power he may bring to fruition your every desire for goodness and your every deed prompted by faith. (2 Thess. 1:11)

Grace and peace and all my deep love for you,
Kendra

Acknowledgments

Goodness, where do I even start? Part of me wants to begin by thanking my elementary teachers for teaching me to read and write. But then I realized going back that far would keep us here until 2057 AD. (But seriously, thank you, elementary teachers.)

So instead I'll start with you, dear reader: from the bottom of my heart, thank you for taking time to read the words that I, and many others, have worked so hard to craft into this book. The fact that you gave of your time to listen to me talk about stuff that is dear to my heart makes me truly happy. Some of you have been reading stuff I have written since I first started a tiny blog while living in Guatemala. Some of you have been prayer warriors and emotional support and friends to laugh with as I overshare on social media. Some of you are my beloved Launch Team that I'm pretty sure I would take a bullet for. And some of you are meeting me here for the first time. Either way, *thank you*.

To my agent, Tamela Hancock Murray, and the Steve Laube Agency, I can't say this enough: thank you for taking a chance on me. Tamela, even when I first submitted my book proposal and the answer was "not yet," you took the time to offer guidance and to encourage me in the right direction, and I am forever grateful. You are the best advocate and cheerleader I could ask for.

Also, a huge thanks to the team at Thomas Nelson. Thank you for believing in the message of this book, even when we took a millennium to land a title. Joel Kneedler, Meaghan Porter, and Elisabeth Sullivan: you are magicians. I am so grateful my first manuscript didn't make you close up shop and quit loving words, but that you were willing to work your magic and help make this book the best it could be. Lori Cloud, Judy McDonough, and Kristi Smith: you are brilliant. Thank you for walking me through my shaky first steps of publishing and marketing a book.

And then there are the friends in each place I have lived: Michigan, Iowa, Guatemala, Illinois, and Wisconsin—you make me feel like a millionaire. A special shout-out to Kaylee Sleeman and Shari Meyering for never getting off my back until I attempted to write a book. You were annoying in the absolute best way. Also, to the beautiful people that Husband and I worked next to, lived by, and squashed into microbuses with during our three years in Guatemala and at Inter-American School: you changed our lives and challenged our perspective forever, and for that we are glad.

Rhoda Mattson, you almost gave me a heart attack when you offered to organize a group to read through my manu-script, but I am so glad you asked. Ann Payne, Ann Park, and Rhoda—you three are the wisest of women. Our Saturday-morning gatherings to read and discuss each chapter were the best. By offering your theological and practical feedback, you gave me courage to press forward, knowing I wasn't alone in these thoughts.

And to all the others who read and gave feedback on vari-ous chapters and topics, you are the bomb diggity: Dr. Dave Larson, Pastor Michael Langer, Aubrie Benting, Madison

Potgeter, Mary Verwys, Grandpa and Grandma (Larry and Betty) Potgeter, and Kylie Triola, thank you. (Kylie, I hate cancer. Also, the world misses your contagious smile.)

Trinity Presbyterian Church in Palos Heights, you've got it going on. While these thirty days of stories happened shortly before we met you, your hospitality and community and tender care since then and through our worst of times taught me so much about reckless love. I wish we'd had more than two years together, but I am grateful for those two very important years with you.

To our neighbors in the South Side of Chicago (Josh, Christina, Arie, Roger, Alison, Katy, Metin, Scott, Evelyn, Kate, Pam, Mary, Nadine, Alex, Noah, George, Jim, Joan, and that one guy whose name I never learned but seemed sort of nice)—it was lovely to live by you for two short years, and to share washing machines, a parking lot, and dessert together. You were a blessing. I pray you will know that any bits of kindness we attempted to show you were rooted in Christ's enormous kindness He first showed us.

To my parents, Dave and Renee Potgeter, and all my sibs: I like you, I really do. I know you may not think so after I keep choosing to not live in Michigan, but I promise that after Husband, you guys are the next thing that feels like home to me. Thank you for teaching me to laugh at myself when I achieved body odor at the ripe age of kindergarten. Thank you for raising me with *The Sandlot* and *The Goonies* and a whole lot of Jesus. Thank you for helping me find humor when life can be anything but funny. You guys are hilarious and at times wildly inappropriate.

Next, I want to thank my in-laws, Dan and Karen Broekhuis. In Guatemala they call the butt of a loaf of bread the "mother-in-law," but in reality, you two are all that is good for the soul between the two bread butts. Thank you for raising the kind and generous man I call Husband. And thank you for all the times you drove multiple hours to watch the kids so that I could have precious quiet time to write.

To Baby, who is now Threenager, and to our other Baby: you two are a trip, and I wouldn't have it any other way. I love being your mommy. I want so much for your lives, but most of all I want you to know Christ and His big, beautiful grace. I want your daddy and me to show you that following Jesus is something to be absolutely excited about, the wildest ride of your life. (And to Aliza, our baby in heaven—your short life taught me so much, but I wish you were here.)

Handsome Hubby. Collin. I promised I wouldn't write any acknowledgments for you because you are humble and that would embarrass you, but consider this paragraph evidence that I lied. This book would not be physically typed out were it not for you sacrificing your own downtime to let me lock myself in our room while you wrangled the kids. Let me sum up my millions of mushy thoughts about you by simply saying this: You are the one who keeps teaching me what reckless, selfless love looks like every single day. Toward our beautiful children, our neighbors, the students you teach, and me. You are a hunk.

And, Lord, from the deepest depths of my soul, thank You for this opportunity to do something I love. My prayer is that all these hours of typing all these words will bring You glory. Over the past two years, through times of intense emptiness and times of abundant fullness, You have displayed over and over Your generous love. May we learn to give because You gave. May we love recklessly, just as You demonstrated through Your own life on this earth. I love You.

Notes

Before We Get Started

1. "Martin Luther: Do You Think God Needs Your Good Works?" *Generosity Monk*, accessed February 4, 2016, http://www.generositymonk.com/Generosity_Monk/Meditations/Entries/2012/9/9_Martin_Luther__Do_you_think_God_needs_your_good_works.html.

Chapter 1: Five Quarters and a Tide Detergent Pod

1. Mother Teresa, *Where There is Love, There is God: Her Path to Closer Union with God and Greater Love for Others* (New York: Crown Publishing Group, 2010), 328.

   "A Quote by Mother Teresa," *Goodreads*, accessed February 8, 2015, http://www.goodreads.com/quotes/20324-it-s-not-how-much-we-give-but-how-much-love.

Chapter 2: Mulligan Day

1. C. S. Lewis, *Mere Christianity: A Revised and Amplified Edition, with a New Introduction of the Three Books, Broadcast Talks, Christian Behavior, and Beyond Personality*, C. S. Lewis Signature Classics (New York: HarperOne, 2015), 147–48.

Chapter 3: Introverts Unite!

1. Adam S. McHugh, *Introverts in the Church: Finding Our Place in an Extroverted Culture* (Downers Grove, IL: InterVarsity Press, 2009), 184.

Chapter 4: Instead I'll Say, "I'll Be Thinking About You"

1. Oswald Chambers, "Greater Works," *My Utmost for His Highest*, October 17, http://utmost.org/classic/greater-works-classic/.

Chapter 5: Déjà Vu and the Car That Wouldn't Start

1. Charles R. Swindoll, *Jesus: The Greatest Life of All* (Nashville: Thomas Nelson, 2008), 100.

Chapter 6: Don't Focus on the Family?

1. Francis Chan, "Don't Focus on the Family—Francis Chan," YouTube video, 20:00, from a national Focus on the Family convention, posted by Nate Hanson, January 4, 2011, https://www.youtube.com/watch?v=SKsggQcptnY.
2. Starved Rock State Park website, http://www.starvedrock statepark.org.
3. Chan, "Don't Focus on the Family."

Chapter 8: All I Wanted Was Some "Me Time"

1. Mary Poplin, *Finding Calcutta: What Mother Teresa Taught Me About Meaningful Work and Service* (Downers Grove, IL: InterVarsity Press, 2008), 123.
2. Google search of the words "Me Time", June 22, 2016, https://www.google.com/#safe=off&q=me+time.

Chapter 9: The Name Is Bond

1. Brother Yun and Paul Hattaway, *The Heavenly Man: The Remarkable True Story of Chinese Christian Brother Yun* (Peabody, MA: Hendrickson Publishers Marketing, 2002), 3.

Chapter 10: Mom Brain to the World

1. Tony Campolo, "Is Stephen Colbert a Red Letter Christian?" *Red Letter Christians*, December 24, 2010, http://www.red letterchristians.org/is-stephen-colbert-a-red-letter-christian/.

Chapter 11: Why Apple Crisp and the Fragrance of Christ Smell So Good

1. Michael Langer, "Called to Be Different" (sermon), Trinity Presbyterian Church PCA, Palos Heights, IL, September 13, 2015.
2. Mary Poplin, *Finding Calcutta: What Mother Teresa Taught Me About Meaningful Work and Service* (Downers Grove, IL: InterVarsity Press, 2008), 111.
3. Ibid.

Chapter 12: I'm Still Afraid of the Dark, Among Other Things

1. Tim Kizziar, quoted in Francis Chan, *Crazy Love: Overwhelmed by a Relentless God* (Colorado Springs: David C. Cook, 2008), 93.
2. Nancy Guthrie, *Holding On to Hope: A Pathway Through Suffering to the Heart of God* (Carol Stream, IL: Tyndale Momentum, 2004), 86.

Chapter 13: Starved World

1. Joe Stowell, "More Than We Deserve," *Our Daily Bread*, May 23, 2014, http://odb.org/2014/05/23/more-than-we-deserve/.

Chapter 14: My Affair with List Making

1. Shel Silverstein, *The Giving Tree* (New York: Harper & Row, 1964), 52–53.
2. Darren Prince, "A Late Night Chat with My Dog," quoted in John B. Hayes, *Sub-merge: Living Deep in a Shallow World: Service, Justice and Contemplation Among the World's Poor* (Ventura, CA: Regal Books, 2006), 218, emphasis added.
3. Kendra Broekhuis, "Martha, Martha," *Grace & Peace* (blog), December 8, 2013, http://ckbroekhuis.blogspot.com/2013/12/martha-martha.html.

Chapter 15: One Quarter Short of a Laundry Load

1. Eryn Sun, "Francis Chan: Christians Not Praying How God ntended," *Christian Post*, December 14, 2011, http://www

.christianpost.com/news/francis-chan-christians-not-praying
-how-god-intended-64814/.
2. Ibid.

Chapter 16: Your Breath Smells Like Gospel

1. Michael W. Smith, *Friends Are Friends Forever: And Other Encouragements from God's Word* (Nashville: Thomas Nelson, 1997), 196.

Chapter 17: Don't Be Surprised When He Answers

1. Timothy Keller, *Prayer: Experiencing Awe and Intimacy with God* (New York: Dutton, 2014), 228.

Chapter 18: "Love Ya"

1. Shauna Niequist, *Cold Tangerines: Celebrating the Extraordinary Nature of Everyday Life* (Grand Rapids: Zondervan, 2007), 17.
2. "I've Got 99 Problems," posted by "Walter Virgin," http://www.memes.com/img/3212.

Chapter 19: Past the Scattered Feminine Hygiene Products

1. Max Lucado, illustrated by Toni Goffe, *The Children of the King* (Wheaton, IL: Crossway Books, 1994), 29–30.

Chapter 20: Golf and Power Outages

1. Jen Hatmaker, *For the Love: Fighting for Grace in a World of Impossible Standards* (Nashville: Nelson Books, 2015), 115.
2. Mark Dindal, Robert Lence, Brian McEntee, Rick Calabash, David Womersley, and Kelvin Yasuda, *Cats Don't Dance*, Directed by Mark Dindal, released March 26, 1997 (Turner Home Entertainment, 2004), DVD.
3. Jen Hatmaker, *For the Love: Fighting for Grace in a World of Impossible Standards* (Nashville: Nelson Books, 2015), 115.
4. Ibid.

5. Rachel Jones, "Christian Faith and Minimalism," *Nourishing Minimalism* (blog), September 24, 2012, http://nourishing minimalism.com/2012/09/christian-faith-and-minimalism.html.

Chapter 21: Would the Neighborhood Miss Us?

1. Tim Chester and Steve Timmis, *Everyday Church: Gospel Communities on Mission* (Wheaton, IL: Crossway, 2012), 28.
2. Dave Larson, "They Seemed Like Nice People" (sermon), Hope Christian Reformed Church, Oak Forest, IL, October 19, 2014, used by permission.
3. Ibid.
4. Chester and Timmis, *Everyday Church*, 28.
5. Larson, "They Seemed Like Nice People."
6. Ibid.
7. Ibid.

Chapter 22: Chicken Soup for My Soul

1. Sarah Young, *Jesus Calling: Enjoying Peace in His Presence, deluxe edition* (Nashville: Thomas Nelson, 2010), 131.
2. "The Web of Poverty: Understanding and Responding to Poverty in England," *Church Urban Fund*, accessed May 18, 2016, http://www2.cuf.org.uk/sites/default/files/Web%20 of%20Poverty.pdf.
3. Percentage calculated on "How Rich Am I?," *Giving What We Can*, accessed October 16, 2015, https://www.givingwhatwecan .org/get-involved/how-rich-am-i.

Chapter 23: Give the Gift of Stress This Christmas

1. Hilary Lewis, "Five of the 'Colbert Report' and 'Daily Show's' Best Black Friday Segments," *Hollywood Reporter*, November 28, 2014, http://www.hollywoodreporter.com/news/black-friday -colbert-report-daily-show-752783.
2. Ibid.
3. Kendra Broekhuis, "Christmas: It's Not Our Birthday Party," *Grace and Peace* (blog), December 7, 2014, http://ckbroekhuis

.blogspot.com/2014/12/christmas-its-not-our-birthday-party
.html.

4. Mike Yankoski, *Under the Overpass: A Journey of Faith on the Streets of America* (Colorado Springs: Multnomah, 2005), 219.

Chapter 24: Let There Be Peace at the Magic Tree House

1. *Once a Day Every Day: For a Woman of Grace* (Brentwood, TN: Freeman-Smith, 2012), Day 32.

Chapter 25: Control Enthusiast

1. K. P. Yohannan, *Revolution in World Missions: One Man's Journey to Change a Generation* (Carrollton, TX: Gospel for Asia Books, 2004), 64.

Chapter 26: The Sidewalk of Motherhood

1. Mary Poplin, *Finding Calcutta: What Mother Teresa Taught Me About Meaningful Work and Service* (Downers Grove, IL: InterVarsity Press, 2008), 122.
2. Mary Verwys, *Wednesday Mourning: A Sidewalk Counselor's Journal of God's Grace in the Abortion Struggle* (Grand Rapids: Roberts Publishing Company, 2009), 82, used by permission.
3. Ibid., 71–72.
4. Ibid., 98–99.

Chapter 27: But Do They Deserve My Gift?

1. Kent M. Keith, "Anyway, The Paradoxical Commandments," *The Paradoxical Commandments*, accessed June 26, 2015, http://www.paradoxicalcommandments.com/.

Chapter 28: Open-Soul Surgery

1. Kristen Welch, *Rhinestone Jesus: Saying Yes to God When Sparkly, Safe Faith Is No Longer Enough* (Carol Stream, IL: Tyndale Momentum, 2014), 156.

2. Mike Yankoski, *Under the Overpass: A Journey of Faith on the Streets of America* (Colorado Springs: Multnomah, 2005), 217.

Chapter 29: Where's the Sex, Drugs, and Rock and Roll?

1. Francis Chan, tweeted by @CatalystLeader on Twitter, October 4, 2012, https://twitter.com/catalystleader/status /254016449285353473.

Chapter 30: Too Early for a Pregnancy Test

1. John B. Hayes, *Sub-merge: Living Deep in a Shallow World: Service, Justice and Contemplation Among the World's Poor* (Ventura, CA: Regal Books, 2006), 190.

And Since Then?

1. Dietrich Bonhoeffer, *The Cost of Discipleship* (New York: Touchstone, 1959), 56.

About the Author

Kendra Broekhuis realized the cool thing to do when you move overseas is to start a blog, so when she and her husband, Collin, moved to Guatemala for three years, that's exactly what she did. She has found joy and therapy in writing ever since, and desires to be an encourager to all women honest enough to admit their struggles and celebrate their greatest joys in life. For her day job, Kendra stays home with two of their children, Jocelyn and Levi. She and her family now live and work in the city of Milwaukee, still attempting to learn what Love Your Neighbor is supposed to look like. Kendra's love language is Dove chocolate.

Visit Kendra's blog at www.kendrabroekhuis.com/blog.